Beginning Tap Dance

INTERACTIVE DANCE SERIES

Lisa Lewis, EdD

Austin Peay State University

Human Kinetics

Library of Congress Cataloging-in-Publication Data

Lewis, Lisa, 1959-
  Beginning tap dance / Lisa Lewis.
    p. cm. -- (Interactive dance series)
  Includes bibliographical references and index.
  1. Tap dancing--Study and teaching.   I. Title.
  GV1794.L48 2013
  792.78--dc23

2012026294

ISBN-10: 1-4504-1198-3 (print)
ISBN-13: 978-1-4504-1198-1 (print)

Portions of chapters 1 through 4 are adapted from Gayle Kassing, 2013, *Beginning ballet* (Champaign, IL: Human Kinetics).

The web addresses cited in this text were current as of December 12, 2012, unless otherwise noted.

Acquisitions Editor: Gayle Kassing, PhD; **Developmental Editor:** Bethany J. Bentley; **Assistant Editor:** Derek Campbell; **Copyeditor:** Joanna Hatzopoulos; **Indexer:** Michael Ferreira; **Permissions Manager:** Dalene Reeder; **Graphic Designer:** Joe Buck; **Graphic Artist:** Yvonne Griffith; **Cover Designer:** Keith Blomberg; **Photographer (cover and interior):** Bernard Wolff, unless otherwise noted; photo on p. 95 by Bai Jingshan/Xinhua/ZUMAPRESS.com; p. 98 by General Photographic Agency/Hulton Archive/Getty Images; p. 101 by Frank Driggs Collection/Getty Images; p. 103 by Globe Photos/ZUMAPRESS.com; p. 104 by Tampa Bay Times/ZUMAPRESS.com; p. 105 by Darnell Renee/ZUMA Press; **Visual Production Assistant:** Joyce Brumfield; **Photo Production Manager:** Jason Allen; **Art Manager:** Kelly Hendren; **Associate Art Manager:** Alan L. Wilborn; **Illustrations:** © Human Kinetics; **Printer:** Versa Press

We thank Barfield School of Dance in Murfreesboro, Tennessee, for assistance in providing the location for the photo shoot for this book.

Printed in the United States of America   10   9   8   7   6   5   4   3   2   1

The paper in this book is certified under a sustainable forestry program.

Human Kinetics
Website: www.HumanKinetics.com

United States: Human Kinetics
P.O. Box 5076
Champaign, IL 61825-5076
800-747-4457
e-mail: humank@hkusa.com

Canada: Human Kinetics
475 Devonshire Road Unit 100
Windsor, ON N8Y 2L5
800-465-7301 (in Canada only)
e-mail: info@hkcanada.com

E5483

Europe: Human Kinetics
107 Bradford Road, Stanningley
Leeds LS28 6AT, United Kingdom
+44 (0) 113 255 5665
e-mail: hk@hkeurope.com

Australia: Human Kinetics
57A Price Avenue
Lower Mitcham, South Australia 5062
08 8372 0999
e-mail: info@hkaustralia.com

New Zealand: Human Kinetics
P.O. Box 80, Torrens Park, South Australia 5062
0800 222 062
e-mail: info@hknewzealand.com

In loving memory of my best friend, soul mate, and loving husband, Johnny Van Lewis.

Contents

4 Learning and Performing Tap Dance   37

5 Tap Dance Steps   51

6 Developing Tap Technique   83

7 History of Tap Dance   93

Preface

Beginning Tap Dance is your guide through the world of basic tap movement. Every beginner has a unique starting point on this journey; whether you are a novice or experienced dancer, you will find your place in this book. This book takes beginning tap dance in a refreshing new direction in both academic and private studio settings; the concise explanations help you move from reading time to dancing time without missing a beat. Although no book can take the place of a dance class, this book serves as your practice companion as you learn the basics of tap dance.

Beginning Tap Dance is the result of years of training from some of the best teachers in the business, including Danny Hoctor and Maurice Hines; a lifelong study of kinesiology, biomechanics, anatomy, physiology, and pedagogy; and many mistakes, failures, and corrections in dealing with people. My career in tap dance began in my late teens. At that time, I offset the cost of my dance lessons by instructing children in tap dance at a studio in North Carolina. As my professional dance career progressed, I taught more advanced students in tap and jazz dance. Although my experience with advanced students is valuable, the best experience I received in understanding true beginners was teaching true beginners. When I taught beginners at Middle Tennessee State University, I learned about teaching tap dance to novice dancers, fair skill and knowledge evaluations, and progression. These learning experiences form the foundation of this book.

Each chapter in this book provides you with a framework for developing your skills and knowledge as you evolve into a tap dancer.

Chapter 1, Introduction to Tap Dance, provides an overview of tap dance. It examines what to expect in your first tap dance class, including the definition and the benefits of tap dance, and it explains your role as a student of the class.

Chapter 2, Preparing for Class, provides information regarding what to wear, how to select your tap shoes, mental and physical preparation for the class, and your unique learning style.

Chapter 3, Safety and Health, discusses studio and personal safety, basic anatomy and kinesiology, and preventing and treating common dance injuries.

Chapter 4, Learning and Performing Tap Dance, presents the learning process of tap dance, rhythmic elements, and the artistry of dance.

Chapter 5, Tap Dance Steps, introduces you to the steps of tap dance along with the understanding of movement. Video clips of these steps are available on the accompanying web resource at www.HumanKinetics.com/BeginningTapDance1E.

Chapter 6, Developing Tap Technique, focuses on developing your tap technique, how each part of the class structure is important for development, and how to improve your tap technique.

Chapter 7, History of Tap Dance, demonstrates the uniqueness of tap dance as it relates to the diverse ethnic groups that contributed to this art form. This chapter traces the history of tap dance to forms such as the Irish jig, African dance, and Native American dance.

The web resource that accompanies this book offers supplemental, interactive instruction. Visit www.HumanKinetics.com/BeginningTapDance1E to check it out. This resource provides you with added opportunities to practice the dance steps explained in this book.

As you enter the world of tap dance, keep in mind that this book is just the beginning, offering you a small selection of tap steps from the hundreds of possibilities that exist. Just as each student is unique, each teacher offers variations in names of certain steps and how to teach them, so you may encounter some differences between terms in this book and ones used in your dance classes. This is what makes tap dance so wonderful: to discover that every region inherited its own vocabulary. It is exciting to learn and appreciate those differences, and stick with the ones that work for you. You may want to make notes about the differences and research other regions' tap step terminology. As you gain knowledge, experience, and confidence, you will develop your own path to seek more advanced steps and styles. Enjoy the journey!

Acknowledgments

Special thanks to Bonnie Nemeth and Lizzy Morgan of Barfield School of Dance in Murfreesboro, Tennessee, for the use of their studio and to dancers Jasmine Thompson, Alicia List, Christine Licsko, Korissa Earls, Kalea Barnett, and Savannah Welch for the many hours spent as dancers and models. I would also like to thank Gayle Kassing and Bethany Bentley for their support, advice, and patience through this journey.

How to Use the Web Resource

In a tap class, exercises and combinations can move quickly. They can also contain many new movements or small additions to existing movements you have learned. However, you have an added advantage! Your personal tutor is just a few clicks away and is always available to help you remember and practice the exercises executed in class. You can study between class meetings or when you are doing mental practice to memorize exercises or steps. Check out the book's accompanying web resource at www.HumanKinetics.com/BeginningTapDance1E.

The web resource is an interactive tool that you can use to enhance your understanding of beginning tap technique, review what you studied in class, or prepare for performance testing. It includes information about each exercise or step, including notes for correct performance; photos of foot positions; and video clips of tap steps. Also included are interactive quizzes for each chapter of your *Beginning Tap Dance* text, which let you test your knowledge of concepts, tap basics, terminology, and more.

In a beginning tap class, students learn about tap technique, tap as an art form, and themselves. The Supplementary Materials section of the web resource contains the following additional components for each chapter of your *Beginning Tap Dance* text. These components support both learning in the tap class and exploring more about the world of tap dance.

* Glossary terms from the text are presented so that you can check your knowledge of the translated meaning of the term as well as a description of the term.

* Web links give you a starting place to learn more about a tap work, its style, or companies that present the work.

* Some chapters include e-journaling prompts and assignments to think more deeply about beginning tap class.

* Other assignments include specific activities to apply the concepts and ideas about tap dance.

We hope that the web resource helps you to individualize your learning experience so that you can connect to, expand, and apply your learning of beginning tap dance, enhancing your success and enjoyment in your study of this dance form.

Chapter 1

Introduction to Tap Dance

Tap dance is considered an American dance style with roots from all over the world. From Celtic ring dances to Southern minstrel shows to Broadway musicals, tap dance has a rich history that took thousands of years to create. Over time it has evolved, but the core of this art form remains unchanged. To understand what is at the heart of tap dance, try this experiment: View any video of Savion Glover performing his unmatched tap dancing skills. (You can view a DVD or do an Internet search on his name.) Then, replay the video with your eyes closed. Just listen, and you will understand what tap dance is truly about: creating rhythm. Glover has said that in tap dance, sound is the most important part; in other words, in this form of dance, it is better to be heard than seen.

Many people become interested in tap dance after viewing a video of someone fluttering across the dance floor with rhythmic precision. Whatever has encouraged your decision to explore this dance form, this book serves as a guide through your journey. Do you remember learning how to sing simple songs when you were a child or how to catch or kick a ball for the first time? Tap dance uses the same skills, so you are limited only by your own commitment and persistence. Unlike any other dance form, tap uses the sounds of the feet to create music while incorporating the rhythmic arm and leg movements known as dancing. Most other forms of dance are limited to only the visual input of expressive action. The interplay of the visual movement with the aural rhythms of foot patterns makes tap dance a unique, fun, noisy, and rhythmic form expression.

DEFINING TAP DANCE

Tap dance is an expressive art form using the language of movement and sound. From the moment you first put on your tap shoes, tap dance gives you an avenue to express the inner rhythms that were present in you long before you were born. After birth, you explored your world through touch and movement, which, in addition to your inner rhythms, give you the skills to dance.

To amplify rhythmic sounds, tap shoes are equipped with metal plates you can manipulate by using a combination of heel, toe, sliding, hopping, and jumping movements to create a variety of percussive sounds. These percussive rhythms can stand alone, or they can be used in combination with music. Effectively manipulating these sounds and creating a variety of rhythmic patterns are the defining characteristics of tap dance. The excitement and challenge of tap dance lie in the complexity and speed of patterns along with sound syncopation and expressive performance. Other dance forms focus on body placement and movement; tap adds not only the movement sequence but the mastery of coordinating sounds, too.

Tap dance has a style for everyone, including the graceful, smooth cadence of the soft-shoe, the flashy style of buck and wing, the Nicholas Brothers' own acrobatic swing style, and the stomps and stamps of rhythmic percussion known as *hoofing*.

BENEFITS OF STUDYING TAP DANCE

Why study tap dance? You could ask the same question about learning a foreign language or musical instrument. Tap dance is a musical form of expressing yourself. Poise, grace, creative expression, and appreciation for the arts are but a few reasons for you to study it. Dance in general has many health benefits, including increased **flexibility**, muscular strength and endurance, spatial awareness, balance, and energy expenditure (which can reduce excess weight; Alpert 2011). It also improves mental health by raising endorphin levels, which relieves stress; it reduces anxiety and depression; and it increases self-awareness and self-esteem (Vetter, Myllykangas, Donorfio, & Foose 2011). Tap dance has a place in history, too. When you study how it has emerged over time, you gain an appreciation for history, dance tradition, and world cultures.

You may have tried other dance forms before trying tap dance. Whether or not you have been successful in other dance forms, you can tap dance; in fact, anyone can. You may not realize it, but you have already performed tap steps such as shuffles, taps, heels, and toes while singing or listening to music. You can learn tap dance at any age or ability level. Once you have learned some basic steps, you can create your own variations and combinations of patterns and rhythms. It is as simple as tapping your toes and skipping across the street.

> **DID YOU KNOW?** ▶▶▶▶▶▶▶
>
> Engaging in arts and cultural activities as either a participant or an observer has been linked to higher self-scores of physical and emotional health and well-being (Cuypers 2011).

BASICS OF TAP CLASS

The main objective of a beginning tap class is learning to dance. Thus, the class requires no previous experience and is structured differently from other academic subjects such as literature, chemistry, or social studies. The teacher presents the day's exercises and combinations, then you respond by replicating the movement to music, drum, or any other device that creates a beat. Attending class provides physical practice and intellectual knowledge on which you build your technique and understanding of tap as an art form.

If you have had previous tap dance training, you may be required to attend a placement class where instructors determine your level or you may talk with your teacher about your previous training. Keep in mind that beginning tap focuses on the foundations of tap dance, which may include steps you have already learned. However, if you want to review the foundations to renew your body's movement memory or you simply enjoy practicing the basics, then beginning tap may be the right choice for you. No matter your level, attending class regularly helps you perfect your technique and develop your artistry.

Participating in tap class is a great way to engage both your body and your mind.

Physical Environment

Depending on where you take lessons, your tap class may take place in a room that has many purposes or in a dedicated dance studio. It may be a fairly large room with metal or wooden **barres**, railings that are either attached to the walls or are portable and can stand alone. The room may have mirrors lining one wall, which can be intimidating for some beginning dancers. Eventually you learn to like the mirrors; they become very useful for you and your teacher to see your form and alignment. Usually dance studios have wooden floors that give when you jump and land. Some dance classes are taught in gyms or auditoriums with no barres or mirrors.

Role of the Teacher

Your teacher has many responsibilities, including dictating the major benefits of dance education, communicating its purpose, constructing the curriculum, creating the studio setting, selecting music, preparing for class, creating objectives and student outcomes, performing assessments, understanding learning styles and cues, and teaching students with special needs. The greatest challenge for any teacher is balancing time constraints with class objectives and individual learning styles with technical levels. Your teacher is concerned about safety first, including studio safety and injury prevention (see chapter 3 for further information). Your teacher is also concerned with teaching proper tap technique in an environment that is fun and inviting.

Role of the Musician

Some classes are fortunate to have musicians providing live music. These musicians understand tap dance and know how to work with dancers and dance teachers. In addition to musical knowledge, they have the ability to perform and adjust a steady tempo, ability to follow the teacher's instructions and dancers' movements, and flexibility to adjust as needed to accommodate the teacher's analysis. Most classes use musical recordings with varying tempos. These recordings are preselected and arranged in order. Most combinations are practiced without music until the tempo reaches the correct speed. Most musical selections have an introduction, and the teacher gives you verbal cues for when to begin.

> **DID YOU KNOW?** ▶▶▶▶▶▶▶▶
>
> Dance and music are sister arts. The music in the tap class supports learning about movement and music while it enhances the classroom experience with the synergy between movement and music.

EXPECTATIONS AND ETIQUETTE FOR STUDENTS

As with any class you take, some standard expectations and etiquette protocols exist for tap dance class to be a more productive, safe, and enjoyable learning experience. Your teacher is responsible for providing you with the attendance policy, dress code, and expectations for grading (if you will be graded). Review this information so that you will be prepared from the beginning.

Proper studio etiquette protocols include not talking while the instructor is addressing the class, not chewing gum, and not sitting down or leaving class without permission. Paying attention in class is a must because you are in class to work and learn. Other important class expectations include performing steps as taught and finishing combinations to the best of your ability even if you are having difficulty. If you need clarification on any combination or skill, address your teacher at the appropriate time; do not interrupt the teaching flow of the class.

Preparing and Practicing

You are expected to come to each class prepared, wearing appropriate attire and shoes. Preparation also includes practicing what you learned in the previous class session. Practice time during class is not enough to effectively learn tap steps. You must set aside at least 15 minutes every day to practice new steps and fine-tune steps and combinations that you learned. During class, you must show respect for your teacher and classmates by not cross talking with other students and waiting until the instructor asks for questions. To better prepare for your next class, make mental notes or write down new steps for future practice, find after-class practice partners, and use any resources that your teacher provides. Most dance teachers are available after class or by appointment if you need extra instructions. Take advantage of any extra practice or rehearsal time. Video clips of steps can be very effective while practicing.

Proper etiquette is to stand quietly and pay attention as the teacher demonstrates a step. Save your questions for the end of the demonstration.

Where to Stand

Your teacher may have designated places for you to stand. If not, make sure you have plenty of room to move. Make sure you can see the teacher at all times, and be aware teachers usually rotate lines to give every student the opportunity to be in the front row. Do not move to the back row unless the teacher tells you to move; the teacher wants to observe your ability in order to determine the pace of the class.

Attending Class Consistently

Missing classes means missing opportunities to learn, and it puts you behind in skill development. It may demonstrate the fact that you do not take the class or the teacher seriously. If you have to miss class, contact your teacher regarding skills you missed and find out how you can make up any practice times.

Arriving on Time

Some actions demonstrate disrespect to the class, your classmates, and to the instructor. Arriving late to class is one such action. You should arrive to class at least 10 minutes early to mentally and physically prepare for class. Your teacher may provide you with some pre–warm-up activities to help you prepare for class.

Dressing Properly

Proper attire is a must. Following the dress code allows your teacher to see your movement and make corrections. It also demonstrates respect and that you care about the class and the art form. Keep your hair pulled back off your face, and do not wear any jewelry. Tap dance is a ballistic movement, so proper support undergarments are a must. If you are not sure what to wear, review the syllabus or dress code. Also, being respectful includes attending to personal hygiene. Wear clean clothes, and avoid strong perfumes, lotions, or colognes. Never wear your tap shoes outside on asphalt or concrete, which causes damaging dents. Check your tap screws before each class to ensure that they will not damage wooden floors.

STRUCTURE OF TAP CLASS

The structure of each class depends on the teacher and is therefore unique. The following is one example of how a beginning class in tap dance may be structured.

Pre–Warm-Up

Many teachers expect students to perform a **pre–warm-up** before class begins. Pre–warm-up exercises allow you to prepare your mind and body for class. Some of these exercises include slow ankle rolls, extension and flexion of the feet, lunges, hip circles, shoulder rolls, and easy neck rolls. If you or other students have had past injuries, you may need to give special attention to preparing certain muscles or joints for class. Your teacher can help you come up with the exercises that work best for your needs.

Warm-Up

A warm-up is designed to elevate the body temperature and prepare the body for more strenuous work. Teachers provide appropriate exercises either moving across the floor, standing at the barre, staying in the **center**, or a combination of each. These exercises may include nerve taps, which are performed by striking the floor with the toe tap as quickly as possible to warm up the ankle and the front part of the lower leg. Another warm-up could be performing basic tap steps such as toe–heel, heel–toe, or flap steps while traveling across the floor. As the warm-up progresses, your teacher may have you add hops, leaps, or jumps while performing basic toe–heels, heel–toes, flaps, and shuffles.

Warm-up is a great time to review simple steps needed for more complex combinations. Some teachers include stretching, **isolation exercises**, and locomotor movements in the warm-up. Although light stretches are recommended before more strenuous work, **flexibility exercises** should be performed at the end of class (see Cool-Down, later in this chapter). Light stretches may include simple pointing and flexing movements of the foot, heel raises while balancing on the ball of the foot, or toe raises while balancing on the heel of the foot. Isolation exercises focus on isolating specific body parts, so they can be beneficial for developing **body awareness**, control, and **coordination**. These exercises usually start either at the feet and move up to the head, or vice versa. They may be part of the warm-up or the center floor technique workout. An example of an isolation exercise is moving the rib cage from side to side while keeping the shoulders and hips still.

Across the Floor

Your teacher may have you perform basic tap steps with locomotor movement across the floor. These steps are performed with partners or small groups diagonally across the floor. You must apply proper class etiquette when performing these exercises: Be prepared to start with your group when the teacher cues you, do not stop performing steps midway across the floor, and when you have completed the steps, walk around to the back of the line.

Technique Work

Your teacher may choose to teach **technique** at the beginning of the class before you become too fatigued. Technique work may include more difficult steps, new steps to be added to a combination, or steps evaluated by a skills test. The teacher may use the *see, hear, do* method of teaching. In this method, the teacher demonstrates the step and encourages you to view (see) the step as a whole, then breaks down the step in simple parts. Next, the teacher focuses on the sound of the step and has you to listen to (hear) each rhythmic component. The teacher provides time for you to either work in groups, pairs, or individually to practice performing the step (do). Some teachers may use the *call-and-respond* method of teaching. In this method, the teacher performs a rhythm by clapping, tapping, or singing (call) and asks you to replicate the same rhythm (respond).

When learning a new step, repetition is key. Sometimes students are not given enough time to learn the step, or they are given too much time and they get frustrated. If you need help or don't know how to use your time efficiently, ask your teacher for help. Asking questions helps you develop skills and receive individual instructions. All students learn dance steps differently; this is the greatest challenge your teacher faces. You might learn more effectively when the teacher sings the syllables, or scats while you dance or ask for counts. You may perform best when you learn the footwork first and then rhythm, or vice versa. There is no perfect or right way to learn new steps; there's just what works for you.

Combinations, Dances, and Routines

A tap dance **combination** is a movement phrase consisting of several steps (Kassing & Jay 2003). A **dance** or dance **routine** is a longer, more comprehensive movement series consisting of several combination phrases that usually last between 2 and 4 minutes. This is the fun part of the class, in which you get to show off what you know. Steps learned in the technique workout combined with other elements of dance demonstrate your technique, coordination, and style.

When teaching combinations, your teacher may use the *I do, we do, you do* method. In this method, the teacher demonstrates short movement patterns several times (I do). Then the class performs the patterns along with the teacher (we do). Finally the class performs them without the teacher either all together, in groups, or individually (you do).

Proper technique is important, but developing a sense of individual style is encouraged. You should carefully observe each intricate step, rhythm, **flow**, position of the body, and the style of the performance. The best way to learn the combination is by actually performing the steps. However, you might try **marking** the steps by slightly moving through the combination or mentally reviewing each step for added practice with or without the music.

Cool-Down

You may be surprised to find out that tap dance is strenuous to your body. Tap dance is a high-impact, high-intensity activity, so sufficient cool-down and stretching are recommended. A cool-down is the reverse of a warm-up; it cools the body's temperature and prevents pooling of blood in the legs, which may cause dizziness or faintness. A cool-down may consist of simply walking around the room, performing light shuffles, or doing heel–toe movements. You may perform gentle stretching at the beginning of class in conjunction with the warm-up, but flexibility exercises are recommended after the tap dance workout. Higher body temperature aids in increasing joint range of motion, and stretching helps fatigued muscles to reestablish resting length and reduce soreness and spasms.

To improve flexibility, you should perform static stretches of each major muscle to the point of mild discomfort for 10 to 30 seconds to give the muscles time to relax and lengthen. Flexibility exercises may include sitting and touching the toes while the knees are straight (hamstring stretch), standing on one foot while holding the other foot behind the body (quadriceps stretch), and side bends and front bends to stretch the waist and lower back. Your teacher may use stretching time to recap the major objectives or goals of the class, give any assignments, or answer questions. Some traditional dance classes end with the teacher thanking the students (and musician, if you have one) and bowing while the students clap.

THE LEARNING PROCESS

Learning any new skill is a process, which means that it takes time. Hitting a tennis ball, roller skating, and performing a shuffle–ball–change all use motor skill ability. A motor skill is a learned sequence of movements. It occurs in the motor cortex of the cerebral cortex of the brain (Brashers-Krug, Shadmehr, & Bizzi 1996). When you learn a tap skill, you break down every little movement and sound of the step. This is called the *cognitive phase* of learning (Meyer, Qi, Stanford, & Constantinidis 2011). When you determine the most effective or efficient way to perform the step with appropriate feedback, you have reached the *associative phase* of learning. During this phase, you fine-tune the step and train the muscles to remember how to perform the step.

When you practice performing the step correctly over time, the step requires very little thought and becomes more automatic. This is the *autonomous phase*, better known as motor learning or muscle memory. Long-term muscle memory happens when a skill is repeated to the point that it can be performed without conscious thought. When learning tap dance, you begin having already developed the basic skills needed to perform the steps. Most tap steps require basic locomotor skills such as walking, running, jumping, skipping, and galloping. Other basic skills needed to perform tap are balance, agility, rhythm, strength, coordination, and flexibility. Learning tap is a process that builds from already developed skills. Understanding how the body learns tap steps can better prepare you to develop these skills with less frustration and greater success.

Tap dance is not always a natural foot action. To understand this concept, stand up and walk. Notice that the natural foot action is heel to toe, from back to front. Now, try to walk toe to heel, from front to back; it feels unnatural. You have to consciously think about how to perform this step. However, if you practice it this way over time, the brain will lock it into its memory and it would soon feel natural. When you enter your first tap class, remember that you will have to retrain your body to move in a different way. How fast you learn these new movements depends on how much time you practice them, how accustomed you are to learning new movements, and how focused you are in class. You may pick it up very quickly and in turn may assist other peers with steps in class, or you may need more practice before you get it. Either way, if you are willing and patient, you will learn how to tap dance.

APPRECIATING TAP DANCE AS A PERFORMING ART

While tap dance is a physically demanding activity and therefore an excellent form of exercise, it is also an art form. It blends all the cultures that make up the United States. Most of the tap dance you see today was invented in the 1800s and perfected in the 1930s or 1940s. Like today's tap dancers, early tap dancers combined tap with other dance forms. And like other dance forms, tap is limited only by the creativity of the artist, so it will continue to evolve. Taking a historical look at tap dance can teach you how dancers have used it as a form of communication and reflection of their society, and viewing the beauty of tap dance can involve the brain processes in the analysis of sensory stimuli.

Whether this is your first dance class or you are majoring in dance, you will benefit by attending dance concerts, watching musicals, or by watching movies that focus on tap dance. It is to your advantage to see what great tap dance looks like and strive to perfect your style. It will help you decide what style you prefer, how you can re-create this style, and how you can communicate this style in a dance appreciation class or in casual conversation.

ACTIVITY ▶▶▶▶▶▶▶▶▶▶▶▶

View and Compare

Research videos of the film *Broadway Melody*, where Fred Astaire and Eleanor Powell's smooth, simple, highly rhythmic footwork formed a style that perfected the upright, delicate swing manner of tap dance. Compare their style with Savion Glover in the modern *Happy Feet*, where the light, delicate balls-of-the-feet style is transformed into the heavy, heel-stomping, hoofing style.

SUMMARY

Tap dance is a living element of its practitioners; it is constantly evolving. By selecting this art form, you are in great company; some of the greatest performers of all times tied their tap shoes for the first time and began to experience what it was like to *talk* with their feet. You may or may not become the next tap dance star, but one thing is for certain: Learning tap will enrich your life.

To find supplementary materials for this chapter such as learning activities, e-journaling assignments, and web links, visit the web resource at www.HumanKinetics.com/BeginningTapDance1E

Chapter 2

Preparing for Class

In the Broadway musical *A Chorus Line*, the character Mike sings of his experiences as a child watching his sister tap dance. In the lyrics he sings, "I can do that." Finally, one day he grabs his sister's tap shoes and stuffs them with socks because his feet are too small. When he gets to dance class he proves that he can do that. Mike was successful in dance, but every great tap dance performer has a first day of class.

In this chapter you will learn about proper tap dance class attire and how to select the right shoes to prepare for tap dance. Foot care and personal hygiene are also important components of preparing yourself for class. This chapter describes health-related fitness such as cardiorespiratory endurance, muscular strength and endurance, flexibility, and body composition as well as skill-related fitness such as agility, balance, coordination, power, reaction time, and speed. Mind–body preparation is also addressed, including spatial sense, movement patterns, and kinesthetic sense.

DRESSING FOR CLASS

In most tap classes, students are free to select their own attire. However, some teachers have a dress code, so ask about it before your first class. Tap is a high-impact activity, so undergarment support is highly recommended for both men and women. Women can find dance or sports bras at many sport or dance retail stores. Dance belts are recommended for men. Similar to jock straps, dance belts are designed especially for dance. They protect genitals, and they eliminate visible lines under tights.

Usually people wear jazz pants, yoga pants, or sweatpants with a T-shirt for tap dance. However, some studios require leotards and tights. Regardless of what you wear, allow for proper fit, support, comfort, and ample freedom of movement. Jeans and other street clothes made with stiffer fabrics are never recommended and may restrict movement. Before class, remove jewelry to ensure safety for your jewelry, yourself, and other dancers. Also for safety reasons, pull your hair back and secure it away from the face, even if your hair is short.

These students are properly dressed for class with comfortable, well-fitting clothing, tap shoes, and hair pulled back.

FOOT CARE AND PERSONAL HYGIENE

Tap class gives the feet an intense workout, so dancers' feet require specific care. Always keep your feet clean and smooth. If your feet have corns, calluses, or rough spots, use a foot soak and regularly massage foot cream on your feet to help soften the skin. Keep your toenails clipped to an appropriate length—long enough to avoid ingrown toenails and short enough to avoid discomfort. When you clip them, cut straight across.

As with any physical activity, good personal hygiene is a must. Always wear deodorant. If possible, shower immediately after class and pack an extra towel in your dance bag. Taking a hot shower not only cleanses your body but also refreshes you and soothes aches and pains from strenuous activity. If showering immediately is not an option, change into clean, dry clothes to avoid chafing and odor.

CARRYING DANCE GEAR

Use a dance bag to carry your clothes, shoes, and other items to and from class. You can find bags designed specifically for dance gear at dance apparel stores and online, but gym bags work well, too. Bags can become heavy when they contain a collection of stuff you rarely need or use, so make wise choices about what you need for before and after class. Items to consider include the following:

- Sweat towel
- Deodorant
- Adhesive bandages
- Manicure scissors or toenail clippers
- Safety pins
- Hair clips, pins, ponytail holders, hairnets, and headbands
- A separate bag for wet or used practice clothing
- Personal grooming items and extra towel if you plan to shower after class
- Water bottle and light snack for after class

After class, it is easy to dump your wet dance clothes and shoes into your dance bag, zip it, and go. If your tap class is early in the day or the weather is warm, separate your damp practice clothes from your shoes and other items in your dance bag. Remove the damp items, air out your shoes, and leave your dance bag open before packing for your next dance class.

SELECTING TAP SHOES

Tap dancers wear special shoes equipped with metal plates, called taps, screwed into different styles of shoes (see figure 2.1). Although these shoes can be expensive, they are recommended for the complete tap experience. You can expect to pay from $35 to $100 or more for a pair of tap shoes. Your first pair should be moderately priced and experimental until you decide what you really need. Talk with your teacher, other tap dancers, and tap shoe professionals before you make your purchase.

Many students have tried to glue taps to regular shoes or even athletic shoes, but there is no substitute for a great pair of tap shoes or for using a professional to attach taps to your street shoes.

DID YOU KNOW? ▶▶ ▶ ▶ ▶ ▶ ▶ ▶

Tap shoes may be purchased at dance supply stores or online. If you are buying your first pair, it is best to try on the shoes first to ensure a proper fit. When fitting tap shoes, wear the same type of socks that you will wear in class, practice, or performance, and be sure to walk around, stretch, and perform some tap steps.

Tap shoes come in leather, canvas, plastic, or even sneaker styles. Soles, which can be leather or suede, can be split or whole, providing flexibility or full support. Men's tap shoes are usually black-tie oxfords while the women's vary between oxfords, Mary Janes, or two-tone spectators. Several manufacturers of tap shoes have been in business for many years; Capezio, Bloch, Leo, and Giordano are the most popular.

Your tap teacher may specify what type of tap shoe you should purchase. Not all tap shoes are the same. Split-sole shoes may be very comfortable, but it may be difficult to execute certain toe turns in them because of the lack of arch support. Sneaker-type tap shoes are strong, but they are heavier and carry more bulk. This may be problematic when executing small, quick steps. Most teachers teach a variety of styles; understanding those styles will assist you in selecting the right shoe.

Figure 2.1 Various styles of tap shoes.

When purchasing tap shoes, how they sound is just as important as how they look and feel. Several types of taps are available. The most popular are by Capezio: the teletone, duotone, and supertone (figure 2.2). Of these, the Capezio teletone, which has three screws in both the toe and heel tap, is the most commonly worn. Bloch, Leo, and Danskin are other companies that supply taps for shoes as well. Some tap dancers prefer to glue the taps on their shoes instead of using screws. Every tap dancer has their favorite style, and it is suggested to view as many brands as you can to determine which tap is best for you. Your instructor may require a certain brand or style. Each possesses a distinct sound. You can adjust the sound of your taps by tightening or loosening the tap screws.

Comfort and fit is important, and tap shoe sizes may be different than sizes for regular street shoes. It is best to select a shoe that fits snugly because they will stretch. If shoes do not fit properly, tap sounds will not be as clear.

Figure 2.2 Tap shoe heels: teletone (left); duotone (middle); and supertone (right).

PREPARING YOURSELF MENTALLY AND PHYSICALLY

Dressing for class helps you attain the appearance of a dancer, but it is only part of preparing for class; you also need mental and physical preparation. To give yourself adequate time to prepare your mind and body for class, make a habit of arriving to the studio early.

Mental Preparation

Being mentally prepared for class is as important as having the right attire and shoes, especially if this is your first dance class. Understanding class expectations, class structure, and how you learn can provide you with a less stressful environment. Whenever you learn something new, you create stress in your life. This is considered healthy stress, or *eustress,* and it is needed to develop new skills and improve performance. However, your personal approach and perception to this learning experience can be a negative experience if your learning environment is not conducive to your style of learning. Do you learn better when the whole step is presented first and then broken down, or when smaller chunks are gradually introduced? Do you learn best when information is presented auditorily, visually, or tactilely/kinesthetically (performing the steps)? Either way, you must share your preferred learning style with your teacher, who can provide you with the most effective learning environment.

Sport psychologists recommend using imagery as a way to improve the quality of training sessions (Jeannerod 1994). You can use imagery to mentally rehearse the tap steps, or *image,* before you execute them, thereby significantly improving the quality of your training. When you practice in your mind, observe the details of sensation, such as how your feet feel in your shoes as you strike the floor, the sound of the taps, the vibrations of the rhythm on your feet, and even the smell of the studio. Imagine yourself within your body, not from a remote or onlooking position. Practice, watching videos or professionals performing the steps, observing your performance on video, and imaging will significantly improve your technique.

Your stress level affects your performance and learning ability. Too little stress causes boredom, and too much stress causes lack of focus and more frustration. You can monitor your stress level by using class reflections or journals. If you notice that the class structure or expectation is causing too much stress, talk to someone about it and seek one of the many stress management techniques available, such as relaxation, breath control, yoga, progressive muscular relaxation, imagery relaxation, and positive thinking.

Physical Preparation

Tap dance is a wonderful physical activity that can improve physical fitness. Physical fitness can be related to motor skill or to health. **Health-related fitness components** are cardiorespiratory endurance (aerobic), muscular strength and endurance, flexibility, and body composition. **Skill-related fitness components** consist of coordination, agility, balance, power, reaction time, and speed.

Cardiorespiratory Endurance

Cardiorespiratory endurance is the ability of the lungs, heart, and blood vessels to deliver oxygen to all the cells in the body. It is one of the most important components of physical fitness and the best indicator of overall health. Cardiorespiratory endurance, or aerobic, exercises include walking,

---

ACTIVITY ▶▶▶▶▶ ▶▶ ▶▶▶▶▶

Assessing Your Posture

Developing good posture leads to efficient movement and a healthy living habit. To help you establish and maintain good posture habits, think about posture and do a posture self-check as you go through your daily routine. Check how you stand or walk at different times of the day and in various situations. Just doing three to five checks a day alerts you about your posture and reminds you to think about posture as you walk or stand.

jogging, and swimming; these exercises are at lower intensity with longer duration. Tap dance is not considered an aerobic exercise because most tap dance routines are at high intensity with shorter duration (e.g., a 3-minute dance routine).

Muscular Strength and Endurance

Muscular strength is the ability of the muscle to exert maximal force against a resistance, whereas **muscular endurance** is the ability of the muscle to keep repeating force over time. Tap dance improves muscular endurance by forcing muscles to do repeated contractions. This also improves muscle tone, tendon and ligament strength, and bone density, which improve individual physical capacity.

Flexibility

Flexibility is the ability of the joint to move freely through the full range of motion. Flexibility is important in tap dance, so tap dancers must incorporate flexibility exercises into their workouts. Muscles have elastic properties and respond to stretching by temporarily lengthening. Although joint capsules, ligaments, and tendons are not elastic, with proper stretching they can permanently lengthen and increase in range of motion. Keeping an appropriate joint range motion can enhance quality of life and improves tap dance technique. Always use proper technique when stretching any muscle so as not to overstretch to the point of injury.

Body Composition

Body composition is the muscle, fat, bone, and other tissues that make up the total weight of a person. In the past, doctors and trainers used height–weight charts to determine recommended body weight for optimal health. However, determining how much of the total body weight is fat can give people a more realistic and healthy body weight target. Body composition can be determined through hydrostatic or underwater weighing, skinfold thickness, girth measurement, bioelectrical impedance, and air displacement. To determine your body composition, seek the help of a professional.

Skill-Related Fitness

Tap dance requires successful motor performance. However, with practice, these skills can be improved:

Agility—Ability to change body positions and directions.

Balance—Ability to maintain the body in proper equilibrium.

Coordination—Integration of nervous and muscular systems to perform harmonious body movements.

Power—Ability to produce maximum force in a short period of time.

Reaction time—Time required to initiate a response to a stimulus.

Speed—Ability to propel the body from one place to another.

Mind–Body Preparation

In tap class you focus on physically executing movement sequences while applying proper technique. When you practice coordinating multiple elements in time to the music, you engage in an external and an internal self-checking process. Therefore, your mind and body need to work together as a unit.

Gaining Spatial Sense

As a beginning dancer, you should develop **spatial sense** to tell where your body is and where its parts are in space. Tap directions are more complex than simply front, side, and back. Arm and leg directions have direct relationships to body parts, and the whole body has a relationship to the space surrounding it. Further, the relationships change as you move through space, so you need to develop an acute spatial sense. Spatial sense contributes to your awareness of body line, a key concept in classical tap dance.

Seeing Movement Patterns

When you keenly observe movements in class, you can recognize patterns in them. This mindfulness helps you to memorize movement sequences. One exercise or step can include many parts. When you observe your teacher demonstrating a sequence, first see the body as a whole, then focus on the parts that are moving or nonmoving.

Developing Your Kinesthetic Sense

In dance, as in other arts, you use your five senses. However, the focus often moves quickly from one sense to another. **Kinesthetic sense** is defined as muscle, bone, and joint sense.

As a beginning dancer your visual understanding of a particular movement is primary; it helps you replicate that movement with your body. Next, your aural sense is applied when you replicate the movement in relation to the timing and the music. Developing a feeling for your body's parts and their relationships to each other is key to a kinesthetic sense. As you gain experience in dance, you develop this sense of body–joint positioning. To advance as a dancer, you must learn to transfer your visual perception of correct position or movement to an internal feeling with which you just know what is correct. These levels of learning take time, so have some patience with yourself and your unique movement learning curve.

SUMMARY

This chapter provided information on preparing for your experience in the tap dance class. Dressing for class was covered, including selecting proper clothing and shoes and making sure you take care of your feet and personal hygiene. Concepts of pre–warm-up, warm-up, stretching, and isolation exercises and class technique were introduced. Tap dance is physically and mentally demanding and provides an overall benefit to promote a sense of well-being, so physical and mental preparation were also included.

Understanding your role as a student and making a commitment to class preparation, mental and physical practice, and effective communication with your teacher can enhance your learning and make your experience with tap dance more fun and rewarding.

To find supplementary materials for this chapter such as learning activities, e-journaling assignments, and web links, visit the web resource at www.HumanKinetics.com/BeginningTapDance1E.

Chapter 3

Safety and Health

Tap dance is generally a fun and safe activity. However, as with any physical activity, related injuries sometimes occur. Understanding safety precautions along with basic movement, nutrition, and anatomy can help you prevent many of those injuries.

This chapter examines studio safety, including creating the best environment to minimize joint and muscle stress and keeping the studio free of injury-causing obstacles. Basic anatomy, proper alignment, and how the body is designed to move are also addressed to further assist in your understanding of injury prevention. Sometimes injuries cannot be avoided, so common injuries are covered in addition to simple first aid techniques to speed recovery. Finally, so that you know how to fuel your body for the strenuous movement required in tap dance, proper nutrition, hydration, and rest are introduced.

STUDIO SAFETY

Most classes are taught in a dance studio designed for tap dance, and some are taught in shared facilities such as a gymnasium. No matter what type of space you are in, safety is an essential consideration. Your teacher is responsible for the safety of the dance space and can provide you with instructions about federal, state, and local codes regarding appropriate emergency and safety situations.

Dance studios are busy places with large groups of people coming and going between classes. For your personal safety and to protect your belongings, you should always be aware of your surroundings and the entrances and exits to the studio. Know the evacuation routes from the studio, locker room, and building, and know where you should go in case of emergencies such as earthquakes or tornado warnings.

Equipment and Storage

Before class, be sure the dance space is clear of any items that are not essential for your class. If you move portable barres during class, store them together at one side of the studio so as not to interfere with center group entrances and exits or pathways across the floor. If you are allowed to bring your dance bag into the studio, store it out of the way of entrances, exits, and class activities.

Climate Control

The climate in the studio affects your health and your overall experience. When a large group of people moves in a studio space, the temperature rises. Ventilation, air conditioning, and fans can help keep the studio air from getting too stifling or stagnant and help keep you from getting overheated.

Floors

The floor is a tap dancer's drum. It is also one of the most important safety concerns. The ideal floor for tap dance is a sprung or suspended floor made of hard wood. Most floors are made of wood laid over concrete, which may cause stress to knees, ankles, and lower back. Your teacher will know what type of floor it is and, if necessary, can instruct you to use caution by limiting continuous impact and intensity. Before each class, examine your tap shoes to ensure that screws and other rough surfaces are not sticking out, potentially causing floor damage. Also, do your part in keeping dance floors clean, dry, and obstacle free. Book bags, shoes, and other items should be off the dance floor and secured in a location that will not cause a tipping hazard. If your teacher allows food and drink in the studio, keep them in sealed containers.

> **SAFETY TIP** ▷▷▷ ▷ ▷ ▷ ▷ ▷ ▷ ▷ ▷ ▷
>
> Always warm up. You should not perform tap dance with cold or tight muscles. Tight muscles in the foot and ankle are less able to absorb the shock of high-impact activity.

PERSONAL SAFETY

When you take a tap class, you participate in vigorous physical activity with as many as 30 other students whose bodies are moving through space, sometimes very quickly. Therefore, you should ensure your personal safety as well as the safety of others in the studio.

Personal safety begins with dressing and grooming for the tap class. It includes dressing in proper clothing and wearing well-fitting shoes (see chapter 2). Clothing should fit close to the body and shoes should properly fit for both length and width.

As discussed in chapter 2, removing jewelry is a good choice for class. As you move, jewelry could cause injury to you or to others.

If you have long hair, secure it in a bun or with a clip. A long ponytail or braid can hit you or other students as you move.

Personal Space

Understanding your **personal space** needs during each section of the class is critical to your safety and enjoyment as well as that of your classmates. Your personal space accommodates leg, arm, and body extensions without entering your neighbors' space. Your personal space surrounds you as you stand in one spot and as you move through the studio space. Your personal space has to share the general space in the studio with other dancers as they move individually or in groups at the barre, in the center, and across the floor.

Dancers spread out across the studio in their personal space to perform the center part of the class.

Personal Health Information

Personal health information is just that—personal information. If you have had an injury, surgery, or chronic health condition that might affect your physical performance or the health of your peers, you are not obligated to tell everyone, but you should tell your teacher. To protect privacy, usually teachers encourage students to see them after the first class. Your teacher should be aware of any chronic condition or disease such as asthma, diabetes, or epilepsy in order to be prepared for a possible emergency.

SAFETY TIP ▷▷▷▷ ▷▷▷▷ ▷▷▷▷ ▷▷

When dancing with others, make a habit of checking your personal space before and during an exercise or combination. In the center, use your peripheral vision to see objects or people outside your direct line of vision.

Continued practice of safety rules helps you stay safe and build confidence. As you become more aware of sharing and moving in the space with other dancers, you may identify and be able to avoid dangerous situations in the class. In turn, this safety mindset contributes to your development of a professional attitude as a dancer.

BASIC ANATOMY

Before you can understand movement in dance, you must understand the structure and function of the body. The bones, muscles, tendons, and ligaments are the foundation of movement. The following is a brief description of the skeletal and muscular system.

Skeletal System

Just like an automobile, your body is supported with a frame, or skeleton (see figure 3.1). The human skeleton has 206 bones, which assist in voluntary movement and protect vital organs (Clippinger 2007). It is divided into the **axial skeleton** (central upright axis), which includes the skull, vertebral column, sternum, and ribs, and the **appendicular skeleton**, which is composed of limbs. Many of these bones are linked together to form a joint. There are three types of joints: fibrous, cartilaginous, and synovial. They are classified according to the type of connective tissue that holds them together (Clippinger 2007). **Fibrous joints** are tightly held together so that they allow little or no true movement (e.g., skull). **Cartilaginous joints** are joined by cartilages, which are designed for more of a shock-absorbing capacity (e.g., vertebrae). **Synovial joints** allow for the most freedom of movement (e.g., knee) and are the most common joints.

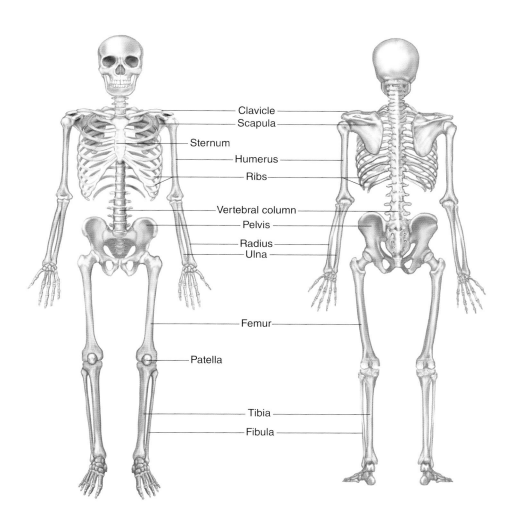

Clavicle
Scapula
Sternum
Humerus
Ribs
Vertebral column
Pelvis
Radius
Ulna
Femur
Patella
Tibia
Fibula

Figure 3.1 The skeletal system.

Muscular System

Movement could not take place without muscles. The muscular system is a network of tissues that produce tension on the bones in order to produce joint movement (see figure 3.2). These actions propel the body through space using the contraction and relaxation of muscles. Skeletal muscles attach to bones and account for up to 40 percent of body weight (Clippinger 2007). Ligaments link bone to bone, and tendons attach muscle to bone. The body has 434 muscles; 75 pairs are responsible for movements of the body. The names of these muscles have their roots in Latin or Greek.

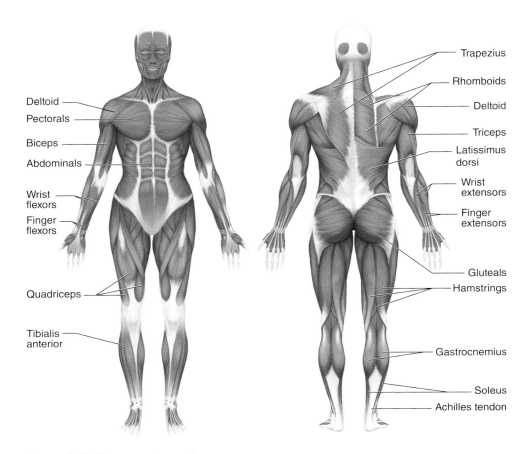

Deltoid
Pectorals
Biceps
Abdominals
Wrist flexors
Finger flexors
Quadriceps
Tibialis anterior

Trapezius
Rhomboids
Deltoid
Triceps
Latissimus dorsi
Wrist extensors
Finger extensors
Gluteals
Hamstrings
Gastrocnemius
Soleus
Achilles tendon

Figure 3.2   The muscular system.

Dynamic (isotonic) muscle contraction occurs when the length of the involved muscle changes (Baechle & Earle 2003). Two types of isotonic contractions occur (see figure 3.3): **concentric** (shortening of muscle and visible joint movement) and **eccentric** (tension involved in the lengthening of muscle). Muscles work together to produce a given movement, each with a different role. When contracted, a mover, or agonist muscle, produces the desired joint movement. The antagonist muscle produces an action opposite of the mover. It usually relaxes while the mover contracts. The stabilizer supports the body part against forces related to muscle contraction. Muscles must work together to provide precise, smooth movement.

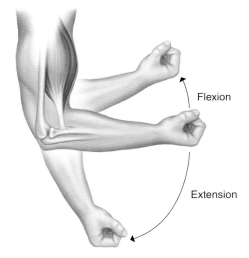

Flexion

Extension

Figure 3.3   Flexion of the biceps is a concentric muscle contraction; extension of the biceps is an eccentric muscle contraction.

BASIC KINESIOLOGY

More dance injuries result from overload and biomechanical factors than from acute trauma (Clippinger 2007). Understanding basic kinesiology, or human movement, can help heal or prevent dance injuries. This section familiarizes you with terms that relate to movement. Dancers and other athletes need to understand these terms in order to better communicate movement injuries or concerns with physicians, physical therapists, athletic trainers, or massage therapists. Also, understanding how the body moves in proper terms will make you a more informed dancer and professional.

Anatomical Position

To understand movement, you must first understand basic anatomical terminology. The universal starting position used to describe movement is called the **anatomical position** (figure 3.4). It is an erect standing position with the feet forward, the arms down by the sides, and the palms forward with the thumbs pointing outward and fingers extended. The **prone position** is lying facedown on the stomach, and the **supine position** is lying faceup on the back.

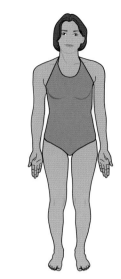

Figure 3.4   Anatomical position.

Joint Movements

Movement occurs at the joint about the axis of rotation within a plane (see figure 3.5) (Clippinger 2007). Synovial joints permit these basic joint movements: flexion (decreasing joint angle) and extension (increasing joint angle), such as

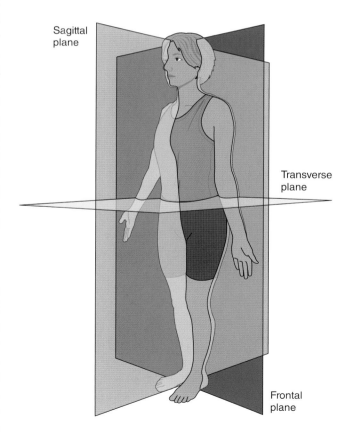

Sagittal plane

Transverse plane

Frontal plane

Figure 3.5   Planes of the body.

bending and straightening the elbow (figure 3.6a), hyperextension (extending past natural position, such as bending backward), abduction (moving away from the midline), adduction (moving toward the midline; figure 3.6b), rotation (external, or turning the anterior surface outward; and internal, or turning the anterior surface inward), and circumduction (movement that creates a complete circle; combines flexion, abduction, extension, and adduction; figure 3.6c).

Joint stability is the ability of a joint to withstand mechanical shocks or movements without injury (Clippinger 2007). The following provide joint stability: the shape of the component part, ligaments as they guide joints through the range of motion, vacuum created in the joint, and extensibility of the muscles and tendons.

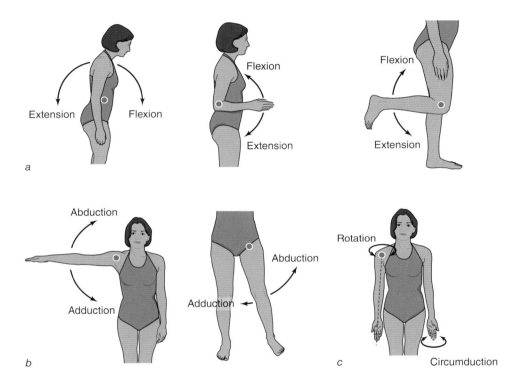

Figure 3.6   Joint movements: (a) flexion and extension, (b) abduction and adduction, and (c) rotation and circumduction.

PREVENTING AND TREATING COMMON DANCE INJURIES

Every physical activity comes with risk of injury. Acute and chronic injuries can occur for many reasons, including lack of body awareness, poor dance technique, overuse of certain muscles, attempting advanced technique too quickly, lack of appropriate warm-up, and studio or floor hazards. The first step to preventing injuries is to practice correct posture, muscle use, and body awareness. Strictly follow the advice of your instructor on ways to properly execute each step. Acute injuries usually occur from landing incorrectly from jumps or leaps and rolling the ankle. Most injuries that occur from tap dance are in the lower extremities (from the hips to the toes) and may include soft-tissue and musculoskeletal damage. The most common injuries in beginning dance classes are blisters, strains, and sprains.

Blisters

Blisters result from shoes that may be too tight or rub the heel or a toe. Blisters can become infected, so take steps to prevent and treat them.

Before you enter the studio, ensure that your shoes have a snug yet comfortable fit. If you get a blister, do not try to pop or peel it; keep the skin on the blister. Keep the feet clean to avoid infecting the blistered area. When dancing, cover the blister with a soft adhesive bandage to avoid irritation. Exposure to air accelerates healing, so outside of class, wear shoes that allow air to get to the blister and at night, leave it uncovered.

Strains

Strains are injuries to muscles or to tendons, which connect muscle to bone. Strains are common; they come with the territory of any physical challenge. If you have never used a set of muscles or body parts specific to the movement you are learning in class, or if it has been a long time since you have taken a dance class, be prepared to experience some soreness in your body.

To avoid strains while you are learning or practicing new exercises and steps, try to execute movement within your range and know when to stop. Doing too much strenuous exercise or too many repetitions is in line with the adage *no pain, no gain*. However, a better strategy is to slowly increase the number of repetitions and the intensity of the exercise to gain with less pain and more longevity. For example, beginning dance students execute most leg extensions at about 45 degrees or lower. Extending a leg to 90 degrees may be a long-term goal, but you should not start there. Start low, then gradually move higher as you gain the strength, flexibility, and control to do the movement.

Sprains

Sprains are injuries to ligaments, which connect bone to bone. Landing on the foot incorrectly from a jump can create a sprain, so pay careful attention to proper landing technique when jumping. Sprains occur in varying degrees. They are more severe than strains and can reoccur if not treated properly. If you endure a sprain, you may notice swelling and bruising in the affected area. To determine the severity of a sprain, treatment options, and the recovery time needed, consult a physician.

Using the PRICED Method

A common treatment for activity-related injuries to the soft tissue such as strains or sprains is the **PRICED** method—**p**rotection, **r**est, **i**ce, **c**ompression, **e**levation, and **d**iagnosis. Your physician might prescribe it to you, or you can decide to use it on your own even if your injury is minor. It can be helpful in healing and also in determining the severity of your injury. Use the PRICED method as follows:

* *Protection.* Move away from possible danger.
* *Rest.* Stop dancing so that the injury can heal properly. You must rest so that you can recover before you return to dancing. If you are in severe pain while resting, consult a physician.
* *Ice.* To reduce swelling, which is uncomfortable and can slow healing, place an ice pack on the injured area several times a day. Place the ice on for 20 minutes, then remove it for 20 minutes before placing it on again.
* *Compression.* To help reduce swelling, constrict the injured area by wrapping it with an elastic bandage. Compression does not mean you should wrap it as tightly as possible. If you feel throbbing, unwrap the bandage and wrap it again more loosely.
* *Elevation.* Raise the injured area above the heart to help reduce swelling.
* *Diagnosis.* If the injury seems severe, see a health care professional.

Adapted from International Association for Dance Medicine and Science, 2010, *First aid for dancers.*

Warming Up and Stretching

In addition to using correct technique, properly warming up and stretching can help prevent injuries in tap class. In addition to physical benefits, doing a personal warm-up can give you time to clear your mind so that you can focus in class. When your mind is focused on the task at hand, you are less prone to accidents. You may need an additional warm-up before class begins because you have had an injury and the affected body part needs extra attention. Or, you may need it because the outside temperature is extremely cold and you need to safely prepare your body for the class; cold muscles are more prone to injuries. In addition, you might want to stretch your muscles to improve flexibility.

Your teacher can help you create a personal warm-up and stretching program, or you can create one based on what you have learned in class. In general, you should begin your warm-up with simple movements in the hips, ankles, feet, and spine and then slowly start to stretch the legs and torso. To increase flexibility, increase your range of motion gradually each time you stretch. Remember, *no pain, no gain* does not apply to stretching. Rather, the reverse is true: Be aware of how your body feels, and recognize the difference between discomfort and pain so that you know when to stop.

Stretching for dance is a continuous, not ballistic, movement. Ballistic movement engages the stretch reflex, which can shorten rather than lengthen the muscles being stretched. Along with any stretching sequence, breathe in conjunction with the movement to deepen and elongate the stretch. Take a deep breath, and as you stretch, slowly release the breath. Slow, controlled breathing relaxes you and assists with the slight discomfort beginners may experience with stretching.

Light stretching before class helps warm up your muscles and can prevent injury.

MAINTAINING GOOD POSTURE

Have you ever watched a house being built? The contractor starts with a strong foundation that is usually made from cement. Then the house is framed directly over the foundation. Finally, the roof is constructed on top of the framed walls. If the frame or roof were not directly over the foundation, the house would be weak and over time could be uninhabitable. That is how the body is designed. Everything must be in alignment in order for the body to move or function properly. Proper posture is necessary for freedom of movement and preventing injury. Dancers should have their posture evaluated by a physician or physical therapist. However, you may perform a self-examination with this simple exercise (Saito, Hanai Akashi, & Neves Sacco 2009):

1. Stand in front of a full-length mirror. Try not to alter your posture in any way. Stand normally. Imagine a straight line from the top of your head through your nose, chin, and navel that ends between your feet.

2. Do you see a difference between the position of each foot? Is one pointing out more than the other? What is the position of the ankles? Are they rolling in, rolling out, or neutral?

- Pronation occurs when the foot rolls inward (figure 3.7), which creates a biomechanical problem and may cause injuries.
- Overpronation or fallen arches happens when you do not give the foot the chance to recover and rest because the foot rolls inward too deeply for too long. Look at the underside of the foot to see if the foot lies completely flat on the ground. This could be a sign of flat feet.
- Supination occurs when the feet roll outward, or become *pigeon-toed* (figure 3.8), which also creates a biomechanical problem and may cause injuries. Usually people with high arches have supinated feet.

3. Look at your knees (figure 3.9). Do they both point in the same direction, and are they directly under your hips? Stand with feet hip-width apart and bend as if you were going to sit down. Do your knees move outward or inward as you sit down? Are your knees straight, knock-kneed or X-shaped (when knees are touching, the ankles are separated), bowlegged or O-shaped (outward bowing of legs), or rotating inward or outward?

4. Focus your attention on your hips. Is your waistline straight, or is one crest of one hip higher than the other? Look at your navel. Is it to one side or on the midline? Is one side of your waist higher than the other?

5. Now look at your shoulders. Do your arms hang evenly? Is one shoulder higher or more forward than the other?

6. Does your head tilt to one side or the other?

7. Turn to the side and have a friend evaluate you from the side. Imagine a line from the top of the head through the ears, shoulders, waist, hip, knees, and ankles. Is your head too far forward or back? Are your shoulders rolled too

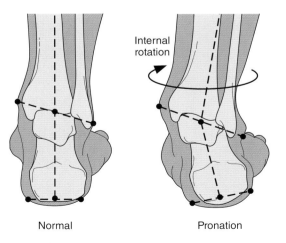

Figure 3.7 *(a)* Normal position; *(b)* pronation.

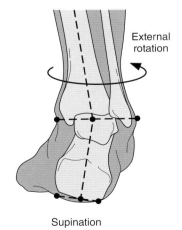

Figure 3.8 Supination.

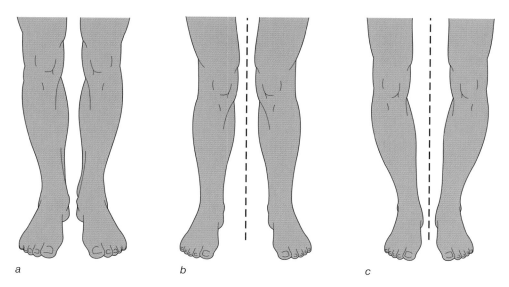

Figure 3.9   Alignment differences in the knee: *(a)* normal; *(b)* knock knees; *(c)* bowlegs.

far forward, or is your pelvis tilted forward or back? Bend over and have your friend palpate (examine by touching) your spine. Is your spine straight or curved? If your spine is curved sideways, you may consider being examined by a physician for scoliosis, a sideways curvature of the spine.

Proper posture is necessary for proper movement and injury prevention. A series of strength and stretching exercises can correct most posture deviations. For more extreme deviations, physical therapy may be recommended.

UNDERSTANDING FITNESS

Tap dance is an art form and a physical activity that requires both physical and mental fitness. In tap class, your movements raise your body temperature and you experience a physical workout. While your body works out, your mind prepares you for your next movements, solves problems, records new spatial and kinesthetic information during your execution, and retains a movement memory for you to review and analyze to prepare for the next class. Understanding the relationship between tap dance and fitness can help you enhance your health for better tap dance performance and enhance your tap dance performance for better health.

Principles of Fitness

Principles used in fitness and sports also apply to dance. The **FITT principle**—**f**requency, **i**ntensity, **t**ime, and **t**ype of activity—and the **overload principle** can help in creating an appropriate exercise program that progresses safely. They are described as follows:

◆ *Frequency.* Most academic tap classes meet several times a week with usually one day in between. The day or time in between gives your body time to rest and recuperate before undertaking the same type of strenuous activity.

◆ *Intensity.* This term refers to how hard you exercise during a period of physical activity. As your tap course progresses, the number and complexity of movements increase to raise the level of intensity.

◆ *Time.* The duration of each class does not vary, but you can vary the length of time you are active during class and the time you practice outside of class.

◆ *Type.* Tap class includes both aerobic and anaerobic activities as well as muscle-building exercises and flexibility work.

◆ *Overload.* This principle refers to working a targeted muscle group beyond what you have previously done in order to gain strength. The body responds to more difficult demands by adapting itself; depending on the type of overload, it increases strength, endurance, or both.

These two principles are related to each other; the FITT principle explains how to approach the overload principle. The frequency, intensity, time, and type of exercise affect how the body is overloaded. Creating healthy adaptations in the body is a slow, continuous process that requires effort; the body must be given time to create gradual increases in strength and endurance.

Strength and Conditioning Considerations

As a dancer, you need a strong core of muscles to augment the work you do in tap class. Sometimes instead of stretching between the barre and the center, dancers engage in push-ups, sit-ups, and other exercises for strength and flexibility. Outside of tap class, Pilates exercises focus on strengthening the core while keeping the body properly aligned, and weight training can increase muscle strength and help to rehabilitate you from an injury. Doing these and other types of activities can help you increase your general health, enhance your dance performance, and avoid or recover from injury.

NUTRITION, HYDRATION, AND REST

Proper training improves dance; the same is true for nutrition. Proper nutrition can improve physical performance for both short-term and long-term health. In order to understand how proper nutrition improves dance performance, you must first understand the basics of exercise physiology and nutrition. Finally, rest is an essential component of dance training and recovery.

Nutrition

Like an automobile, your body requires fuel to move. Movement activity begins with the chemical bonds of food. These chemical bonds are called **macronutrients**, which consist of carbohydrate, protein, and fat. Although protein is important for tissue repair and regulatory purposes, the primary suppliers of energy are carbohydrate and fat. Carbohydrate is digested in the small intestine, absorbed, and then transported to the liver and muscles where it is stored as glycogen. The liver releases glycogen as glucose into the blood stream to maintain normal blood-glucose levels. Glucose is utilized by the brain and skeletal muscles and can function as an immediate energy source. Because carbohydrate is the primary fuel you use during physical activity, it is critical that you consume carbohydrate on a daily basis. Trained athletes and dancers should consume 5 to 10 grams of carbohydrate per kilogram of body weight per day (Dunford 2006).

Proteins are complex organic compounds. The basic structures of protein are a chain of amino acids. They are important for tissue repair and regulatory purposes. Protein-containing foods are grouped as either complete or incomplete proteins. Complete proteins such as those found in animal products (fish, eggs, milk) and some nonanimal products (such as quinoa) contain all nine essential amino acids. Incomplete proteins such as those found in most beans, nuts, and grains lack one or more of these essential amino acids and can be consumed in combination to form a complete protein. Vegans and vegetarians can consume a combination of beans, nuts, and grains to achieve their daily protein requirements. The protein requirement among dancers is the same as for any adult according to the current Dietary Reference Intake (DRI), which is 0.8 grams of protein per kilogram of body weight per day (Dunford 2006). Although many endurance and resistance-trained athletes may need more, dancers usually are not considered endurance or resistance-trained athletes.

Many dancers fear the four-letter word: fats. However, fat is essential; it remains a major energy source, maintains body temperature, protects body organs, contributes to the satiety value of foods, and aids in the delivery and absorption of fat-soluble vitamins. Dietary fat is digested into fatty acids, absorbed in the small intestine, and stored as triglycerides in adipose tissue. These fatty acids can be used immediately for energy.

Hydration

When you are dehydrated, you can feel fatigued, experience lack of concentration, and even be at risk of injury. For peak performance, you must be properly hydrated before, during, and after dance class or performance. To maximize fluid intake, consume water 24 hours preceding training, drink extra water during the 10 to 15 minutes before class begins, and consume water regularly during class. Drink at least 1 pint (500 mL) of water for every pound of body weight lost through exercise. Avoid alcohol within 72 hours before or after training.

> ### DID YOU KNOW? ▶▶▶▶▶▶▶▶
>
> Rethink your drink: Coffee drinks, soda, alcohol, and sugary beverages may be tempting, but they offer little or no nutrition and can even lead to dehydration. Replacing one or more of these drinks with water during the day will rehydrate you and lower the number of empty calories consumed.

Rest

To prepare for dance class, you should be well rested. Along with proper nutrition and hydration, adequate rest supports body recovery and revitalization. When muscles are overloaded, they need rest in order to rebuild themselves. Your mind also needs rest for optimal function. When you don't get enough rest, you become less alert and more prone to accidents. If you have trouble sleeping or are too anxious to rest, learn some relaxation techniques and pace yourself during your day so that your body and mind have time to rest.

SUMMARY

Tap dance is a rewarding and fun activity. This section introduced you to basic anatomy, kinesiology, and injury prevention and care, along with nutrition and hydration information. Understanding the basic terms introduced in this section will enhance communication with your physician, physical therapist, athletic trainer, and even massage therapist while assisting you to better understand your body and how to enhance its health and safety. Tap dance is generally safe, but performing any physical activity includes the possibility of injuries. If you become injured, you should be aware of the type of injury that may have occurred and seek medical advice when needed. Most discomfort can be alleviated using the PRICED method. Your body is your vehicle for movement and expression; understanding how to properly fuel, hydrate, and move it will keep it toned, fit, and less prone to injury.

To find supplementary materials for this chapter such as learning activities, e-journaling assignments, and web links, visit the web resource at www.HumanKinetics.com/BeginningTapDance1E.

Chapter 4

Learning and Performing Tap Dance

Learning and performing tap dance present physical and intellectual challenges; tap dance is a mind–body experience. You have to come to class physically and mentally ready to learn. You use your observation skills to see and hear the movements the teacher presents. As you perform the movements, you monitor how well you understand and are able to replicate movement in time to music. These skills are not perfected the first week you take class; rather, they are acquired over time as your kinesthetic awareness and muscle memory develop. Hence, you repeat exercises and steps but in various patterns and to different music. Repetition hones your technique and performance. The changing patterns and music expand your ability to deal with new elements in relation to the movements you already know.

LANGUAGES OF TAP

Tap uses several languages with which you must become proficient. The first language you learn is that of tap steps. To aid you in learning and remembering the steps, **action words** describe body actions (movements of the legs, arms, and head in a sequence) during an exercise or step.

The teacher uses action words to describe the movement and help you make a connection to the movement. Then you progress to condensing several actions into an exercise or combination. This sequence of movements is represented by a single tap term. When you begin learning tap, the action words in their sequence cue your movements. Later, you can execute a step or exercise without thinking about each movement.

Understanding tap terminology goes beyond translating the movement sequence to recognizing either the spoken or written term. Knowing all these translations comes in handy when it comes to exam time; you may be expected to perform the exercise or step, recognize or write the term, and know its translation into action terms. The vocabulary of tap technique includes positions, exercises, steps, and combinations.

LEARNING TAP STEPS

In tap class you observe while the teacher performs an exercise or combination to music and speaks the action words or tap terms. Then you execute the movement. Listening and remembering the movement sequence coupled with the action words and their tap terms help you while practicing the exercise or combination. Learning new tap steps can be distilled into an easy method: Watch it and hear it, then do it.

Watching

The first step is to watch the movements as the teacher demonstrates them. When you begin to learn tap dance, focus on the starting position of the feet, the actions of the working leg, and the directions in which the leg is moving. Later, when movements include arm positions and traveling, you need to view the whole body doing the movement, what each body part is doing in sequence, and where it is in space. Depending on the style of tap, upper-body movement is not as important as the sound and rhythm of the feet.

Hearing

While watching the teacher's demonstration, you should also listen to verbal instructions—the action terms the teacher uses to describe the movements while executing them. When the music starts, listen to the movement cues spoken in relation to the music. In your beginning practice, the teacher usually cues you when to start a movement. This is your chance to identify which movement takes place on which count or measure.

As the tap course progresses, the teacher demonstrates without the action words and instead uses the tap terminology while indicating the rhythm, count, or measure. Near the end of your beginning tap course, the teacher might say an exercise or combination using tap terms without including a visual demonstration. At this point, you must translate your listening into visualization: You have to hear the tap term, visualize it, hear the sound and rhythm of the tap, and then perform it to the music with the correct rhythm and tempo.

As a beginning dancer, translating the teacher's words into movement is your ultimate goal for learning terminology. While you move from one phase of listening to translating, you likewise gain control of and responsibility for your movement.

Doing

Once you have observed, the next step is to do. When learning a new movement sequence, you usually execute the movements slowly without music, then slowly with music, while the teacher guides you from one movement to the next. As you practice the movement sequence, say the action words or terms to yourself. Continue to execute the movements in their proper sequence and in time to the music, then practice the movement sequence until you become comfortable with it. Be prepared to make adjustments in order to perform the sequence correctly. Remember, at this time you are learning just the basic movement patterns.

During the course, you begin to consider technique, rules, and other elements to refine your performance of beginning exercises. In tap, refining your movement is an unceasing process. After you have the movement sequence in mind, practice it so that both sides of the body can initiate it.

Repeatedly practicing steps at the barre, in the center, and outside of class reinforces learning and helps perfect technique.

Make it a goal to absorb most of the movement presented in class. In some classes, some or many of the components are repeated during the next class meeting. This repetition reinforces learning. In tap, you have to attain a certain level of learning before you can progress to the next level of technique, style, and artistry. Your ability to remember and replicate movement contributes to your progress as a dancer.

LEARNING TAP TECHNIQUE

The beginning tap class is all about learning basic technique, or how to perform a specific step in a consistent manner. Technique involves correct performance as well as incorporation of movement principles. Beyond learning technique, you add timing and quality to movement to develop clarity in performance, conveying a style that radiates musicality and artistry.

Using Cues and Feedback

During class, several strands of feedback can guide your development as a performer. The teacher provides you with cues in various forms as you learn new movement. For example, cues might be in the form of instructions or imagery to help you sense the movement, or they could be rhythmic phrases indicating the timing of a step.

Most often the teacher's feedback is directed to the beginning class to help all students understand the movement or sequence. Sometimes, the teacher gives individual feedback to clarify or extend a specific student's performance. Individual feedback becomes more common during the latter part of the course.

Another type of feedback comes from your personal performance. This feedback can be kinesthetic, intellectual, or a combination. When you execute a movement, you feel how your body is moving and applying movement principles throughout a sequence. While doing the movement, you mentally track the movement timing with the music and the kinesthetic sense of doing the movement, record the experience in your movement memory, and prepare for the next movement—all at the same time. With practice over time, these processes blend to the point where you can be responsible for fine-tuning your performance of the movement.

Putting Movements in Context

Knowing the parts of a movement sequence and timing for a dance step later extends to several steps in a combination. An introductory step, one or more middle steps, and an ending step form a basic combination. Each step in the combination requires clear execution with specific timing and quality.

Memorizing Movement Sequences

As you gain experience in tap dance, the teacher eventually stops cuing your movements using action words and you become responsible for remembering movement sequences. So, you must either memorize the terminology or create your own terms for the movements and repeat them to yourself as you dance. In addition, ask yourself questions such as these:

- Which direction am I facing?
- Which leg is moving?
- In which direction is the leg moving?
- What is the position of my arms?
- In which direction is my body moving?

Repeating action words or the teacher's cues to yourself as you move helps you memorize movement. Learning this technique of self-talk in the beginning can help you integrate other elements such as technique and movement principles in time to the music. Self-talk continues to expand as exercises and combinations get longer and more complicated. Once you can perform a movement sequence, try to execute it without saying the words.

Connecting to Your Kinesthetic Sense

Connecting to your kinesthetic sense requires awareness of your body and its movement. Making this connection takes time and experience; it does not happen overnight. After you have practiced tap dance consistently with awareness for a while, your kinesthetic sense becomes part of the translation process in the language–movement connection; when you hear a tap term, your body just knows what to do and how to do it.

> **TECHNIQUE TIP** ▶▶▶▶▶▶▶▶
>
> Remembering the sequence of movements and visualizing the combination help you learn the combination. Say the action words to yourself to help you remember the combination. Repeat these words while you run the images of the movement sequence in your head to help you string together the movements.

Movement Memory

Movement memory covers information presented in the beginning tap class from the past, connecting it to the present and the future. Movements you perform in class are based on movement memory (also called muscle memory), which connects to developing your kinesthetic sense. This type of memory incorporates continued feedback to the basic movement to clarify the sequence of the legs or alter the arms and head in an exercise or step. Later, movement memory expands as exercises and combinations get longer, contain more steps, and increasingly become more complex. After practicing many repetitions of a movement, you can execute the movement without thinking of the various parts, yet you are able to apply feedback or add stylistic elements to enhance the movement into a more sophisticated performance.

Movement Vocabulary

As you continue to take classes, you gain the rudimentary movement vocabulary of tap. You record your movement vocabulary in a variety of ways: kinesthetic, visual, auditory, and as rhythmic components. You use action words, which are linked to a tap term.

Transposing Movement

To perform tap, you must be able to execute exercises and steps on both sides of the body, or transpose movement. Although one side of your body may respond more easily than the other, the goal is to be able to execute the movement equally well on both sides.

When you perform combinations, you have to move from one direction to another direction. Sometimes a combination moves from side to side, front to back, or back to front. In some parts of the class, you may move across the floor in straight lines or on a diagonal from a back corner of the room to the opposite front corner. Some steps require you turn around yourself or to turn in a circle. Learning to transpose exercises and steps from one foot or side to the other helps to prepare you for moving in various directions.

Mental Practice

Mental practice enhances physical performance. Mental practice is similar to learning by watching, hearing, and doing. Using this technique, you visualize perfectly performing the movements to the music. When you review tap terminology during mental practice, it can support making a movement–language connection, too.

ACTIVITY ▶▶▶▶▶▶▶▶▶▶▶

Meet Your Tap Dance Muse

Imagine stepping into the shoes of a dancer: You are observing, moving, thinking, and feeling like a dancer. When you stand at the barre, move across the floor, or dance in the center, construct a visual image of a dancer performing the movement correctly in front of you so that you can follow that dancer while you perform the movement.

Gaining a Performance Attitude

Gaining a **performance attitude** means that you learn to think, act, and move like a dancer. The first step to gaining a performance attitude is to be able to perform a movement sequence and transpose it to the other side. Once you can memorize a movement and transpose it independently without relying on your teacher to demonstrate it, you can be responsible for your own movement and your teacher can build on your learning in the next class. This independence and acceleration in learning increases your confidence, which leads to developing a performance attitude.

UNDERSTANDING MUSICALITY

Musicality is knowledge about and sensitivity to music. In dance, it refers to how the dancer executes movement in relation to music. Executing movement that is technically correct and in time to the music is the baseline of performance. You begin your study of musicality when you listen to the music while performing movement to it. As you progress, you not only dance in time to the music but also use the music to inspire expression in your movements. As with a kinesthetic sense, with musicality you eventually develop a *feel* for the music and your body just knows how to move to it.

Dancers often use music to help create stories. Tap dancers use foot sound patterns as their storybook. These patterns are transported by impressions of organized sound. Tap dancers become aware of the details of musical structure to improve the quality of the musical experience.

Rhythmic Elements

Musical sound has four properties: pitch (high or low), intensity (loud or soft), tone quality (the medium or instrument), and duration (long, short, or silent) (Evans 1978). **Rhythm** brings music to life; it is defined as measured movement and the timing of notes. Rhythm uses the arrangement of sounds and silences in time. Dancers and musicians can vary rhythms to create the uniqueness of each piece and give each its own character and personality. The basic unit of rhythm organization or pulsation is the **beat**, or **pulse**. The beat measures time. When you dance, you are moving to a beat. Listen to a piece of music and try to concentrate only on the rhythm. Try not to focus on lyrics or individual instruments. Is there a steady pulse? This pulse can be represented visually by a line of individual notes. **Notes** are the symbols that represent the sounds, and **note values** represent the duration of sound (figure 4.1). Regardless of the speed (tempo) of the music, the note value symbols relate to each other.

Whole note

Half note

Quarter note

Eighth note

Sixteenth note

Figure 4.1 Musical note value symbols.

When you listen to music you soon pick up on the fact that some beats sound stronger than others. Throughout the piece of music you will recognize this recurring pattern, which is known as the **meter**. **Accent** is the stress on the beat to make it strong or weak; it gives each meter its own personality. Patterns for meters can be duple meter, triple meter, or quadruple meter (figure 4.2). An accent mark (>) is used to indicate the note that is given the most stress.

Regardless of the meter, the first beat in a measure has the strongest stress, or accent. This is called the **downbeat**. When the accent is not on the downbeat, or on the *offbeat*, the rhythm is syncopated. **Syncopation** includes unexpected rhythms that create an offbeat tune or an interruption of the flow of rhythm. Tap dancers use a missed-beat (sound) type of syncopation in which silence (rest) replaces a beat or sound. This can occur in any measure, disrupting the natural stress of the meter.

Musical **phrasing** occurs when a musical or tap pattern is manipulated so that it separates from the original pattern (out of phase), then rejoins or gets back (in

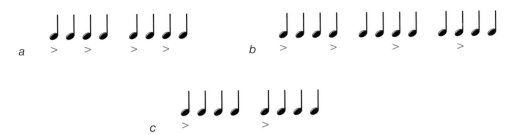

Figure 4.2 *(a)* Duple meter; *(b)* triple meter; *(c)* quadruple meter.

sync). Think of phrasing as two tappers repeating the same steps over and over. One tapper gradually shifts out of unison with the other tapper, creating a slight echo and then coming back in unison.

Musical dynamics refers to the volume (loud or soft) of the music. Tap dancers use this variation, called *light and shade,* to make the sound quality interesting and demonstrate control over the sound. This control of sound with light tapping in contrast with louder sounds also makes for healthier dancers in that they do not bang out each sound hard and heavy, possibly causing foot and knee injuries. In musical notation dynamics are written by using the Italian terms of *piano* (soft) and *forte* (loud). A great example of tap dynamics is Gene Kelly's tap performance in *Singin' in the Rain.*

Have you ever looked at music written down? Some people find reading music to be intimidating. Writers of music have to organize their music for others to read. Music would be difficult to read if the musical piece were not divided into **measures**, which are divided by vertical lines called bar lines. Music is written on five lines and four spaces (figure 4.3). These lines and spaces form a **staff**. At the beginning of the staff there is a symbol called a clef, or key. This indicates the pitch of the written notes. The two most common clefs are the treble clef and the bass clef. When the treble clef line and the bass clef line join, it is called the grand staff. **Pitch**, or the frequency at which sound vibrates, is written on the staff. The higher the notes located on the staff, the higher the pitch.

Tap dance and music are made up of sounds and silence. Duration of silence is expressed by symbols called rests. For every note value exists a corresponding **rest sign**. Next to the musical staff are two numbers, called the **time signature**, or meter signature. Time signature is a notation used to specify how many beats are in each measure and which note value constitutes one beat. The top number tells how many beats are in each measure, and the bottom number tells what kind of note gets the beat.

Rhythm can have an expressive element, which is accomplished by **tempo**, or the speed of the beat. Tempo can be marked with a specific beats per minute (BPM) and can be identified by using a metronome. A **metronome** is a practice tool or device that produces a steady beat. Usually, metronomes play beats between

You're a Grand Old Flag

Figure 4.3   Annotated piece of music.

35 and 250 BPM. Metronomes can be purchased at any music store or online. The following is a list of popular dances with corresponding BPM (Dixon, Gouyon, & Widmer 2003):

Cha-cha	92–137
Jive	124–182
Quickstep	189–216
Rumba	73–145
Samba	138–247
Tango	112–135
Waltz	78–106

If you don't have a physical metronome, you can download one to a personal computer, tablet, or smartphone. Before the metronome, tempo indications or markings were notated in words, which were mostly in Italian. The most commonly used Italian words are as follows (Blood 2011):

Tempo Marking

Presto = quick, fast (>168 BPM)

Allegro = cheerful and quick (120–168 BPM)

Moderato = moderately (108–119 BPM)

Andante = walking (76–108 BPM)

Adagio = slowly (60–76 BPM)

Lento = very slowly (<60 BPM)

Timing and Quality in Performance

Timing and quality of performance are associated with knowing the exercise or step. Determine whether the movement performed is a slow step or a fast step. Recognize whether the movement has a gliding quality or a sharp, striking quality to mirror or contrast the music. As part of the tap class, you practice dancing to various types of music, at varying tempos and time signatures. Likewise, you practice various steps that make up combinations of different or perhaps similar qualities. Learning to identify these and other characteristics of the combination eventually becomes second nature; however, in the beginning class, identifying these characteristics is part of learning basic tap technique. In early beginning tap classes, the tempo of exercises and steps is slow to ensure that your mind and your body understand each movement and the sequence. In steps and combinations across the floor, moving slowly and filling out the music with jumps and leaps helps you acquire both the power and height that you will need to complete when the music tempo gets faster.

Selecting Music

Beginning dancers do not usually select their own music for class. However, exploring various **musical styles (genres)** either for practice or entertainment will benefit you when you become a more experienced dancer. Musical style is musical sounds that belong to a category. Many styles of music exist, including classical, country, soul, rock and roll, hip hop, punk, electronic, and reggae. Seek songs that can complement your feet's rhythm pattern (steps) and tempo. You can choose from

Performing steps and combinations using the proper timing and quality is important, especially when performing as a group.

hundreds of songs, slow or fast. Find music that has sections of breaks, or no beats played, so you can incorporate your own personal sound to the piece. Some songs have percussion only, such as "Planet Drums" or other rhythmic **instrumentals** with no vocals. Seek music from musicals that feature tap dancing, such as *42nd Street, Singin' in the Rain, Anything Goes, Funny Face, Guys and Dolls, The Tap Dance Kid, Crazy for You,* and *Dames at Sea.*

You can find songs popular during the Swing era (1935–1945) from Benny Goodman, Duke Ellington, Glenn Miller, Billie Holiday, Tommy Dorsey, the Andrews Sisters, and Count Basie. Music selection should complement your routine and enhance practice. Songs that are fun to listen to or sing along with may not be the best choices to use while tap dancing, especially for beginners. The best choice for beginners is a steady beat, even phrasing, and a moderate tempo. You can find this type of music designed for fitness or exercise classes. You can purchase it by beats per minute (BPM) with an even 32 counts. Styles come in top 40, classical, classic pop, 60s, 70s, 80s, or 90s, disco, rock, club dance tribal, electro, trance, Eurobeat, swing, Latin, and instrumental. The most important pitch, tempo, and rhythm is the one that is made with the feet, while the choice of music should accent foot patterns.

UNDERSTANDING ARTISTRY

In dance, artistry means being able to express the intent of the dance, the choreographer's ideas, and emotions through movements and gestures. Similar to reading a great poem, seeing a riveting dramatic performance, listening to a piece of music that transports your spirit, or viewing a work of art that connects to your senses, a dance artist visually expresses through the fullness and elegance of movements and gestures in relation with the music that accompanies the performance—the poetry, emotion, and drama of dance. This is what you see on stage when a dance artist interprets a choreographic work. Developing artistry is not studied separately from technique, nor is it studied only in advanced classes. Actually, it starts in the beginning tap class.

Every day as you perform in tap class, the exercises and steps are parts of the bigger picture of studying tap as an art form. While you perform beginning tap combinations, you learn to apply techniques, movement principles, rules, and protocols. These fundamentals underlie aesthetics and performance artistry.

APPLYING AESTHETIC PRINCIPLES TO TAP DANCE

All dance forms share the same aesthetic principles that underlie the arts and function as a basis on which choreographers, dancers, and the audience judge a dance work. In the dance studio, the aesthetic principles as they apply to tap guide the teacher in developing combinations. Students learn to understand and practice applying these principles through performing tap combinations.

The general aesthetic principles that underlie other art forms and dance are shown in figure 4.4. They include the following:

◆ *Unity* is cohesion of all the elements of a combination that make it a whole statement.

◆ *Variety* refers to steps, directions, and levels that keep and hold the attention or even challenge the dancer.

◆ *Contrast* highlights or stimulates interest and adds dimensions to the dance.

◆ *Repetition* is the repeated occurrence of an element that makes it a constant.

◆ *Balance* provides a sense of proportion to the combination that gives it a sense of equality between the parts.

Adapted from Kassing and Jay 2003, p. 370.

These aesthetic principles may seem abstract and disconnected from the movements and steps that constitute beginning tap and its technique. However, after you acquire a working vocabulary of tap and understand movement principles and rules, aesthetic principles come into play so that tap expands beyond being a technical art and becomes an expressive one as well. In order for this connection to become integrated into your performance, you have to gain awareness of the aesthetic principles and how they relate to tap. Integrating the aesthetic principles into your dancing begins with performing tap as an artist from day one in the tap class. When you practice movement

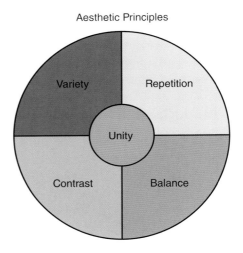

Aesthetic Principles

Figure 4.4 Aesthetic principles support dance and other art forms.

principles, rules, and protocols, they become integrated into your performance and lay a foundation upon which you can layer qualities, style, musicality, and personal interpretation. This is a continuous synergy and development that deepens over time, with practice, and with concerted attention to your physical and mental understanding of tap.

PREPARING FOR CLASS PERFORMANCE TESTING

In an academic tap class, you take two types of tests: written (either on paper or online) and performance. The written test covers vocabulary, action terms, tap terminology, movement principles, rules, and protocols. The performance test involves performing exercises at the barre and combinations in the center. In addition, you may be expected to write response papers and reviews of dance performances.

Generally to expedite performance tests, the entire class performs barre and combinations for one or two class periods. Usually you learn and practice the combinations in class and memorize them for performing with your class or group.

On the day of the performance test, your teacher presents barre and combinations and expects you to execute them from memory. You should practice to ensure that you have the movement sequence and technique correct, you coordinate your movements with the music, and you express the quality of the combination. Use practice strategies to prepare for your test in and out of class. The following questions help you remember combinations at the barre and in the combinations.

- What direction do I face to start?
- What is the starting foot position?
- What is the preparation (foot and arms)?
- What is the first movement?
- What is the sequence of the combination?
- What is the ending?

With practice and experience, answering these questions becomes second nature; the questions function as self-check points in your performance.

Practicing for the Performance Test

To prepare for the performance test, practice the required combinations. These movements become deeply embedded in your movement and intellectual memory. The following steps help you acquire this level of understanding.

1. Practice each of the combinations by yourself until you feel confident.
2. Execute the combinations facing the mirror while you do a self-check for correctness.
3. Practice the combinations facing away from the mirror and do a self-check.
4. Make a list of the combinations you feel confident about and those that require some extra study. Then focus your practice on these specific areas.
5. Practice the combinations with a partner observing you, then observe your partner. Share feedback on each other's execution, and share areas to review.

In a performance test, you must know and be able to perform all the combinations of the performance test. Often during class and performance testing, students follow people in front of them or watch them in the mirror. This practice is detrimental; it confirms for the teacher that you either cannot perform the combination without outside visual help or you have not accepted your responsibility for knowing and performing the combinations.

Between class practices of the test, review the test by mentally visualizing yourself performing and by physically practicing the combinations. Before the performance test, make time to do a mental review of the test combinations. During the performance test, you have to think about the movement you are executing and also think ahead to transitions and to the next movements in the combination.

To perform each movement in the combination, you have to do all parts of it from start to finish fully and with the correct energy level and dynamics. Even if you have prepared for the test and have confidence that you know the combinations, problems can surface during performance. Keep a mindset that if you should encounter a problem or make a mistake, you will keep your performance attitude and complete the combination. Also, keep these ideas in mind:

- Think in the moment, and think ahead.
- Deal with problems, and recover.
- Complete every movement.
- Finish the combination.

Waiting to Perform

While you are standing quietly at either the back or side of the studio waiting to perform the next combination, you have an opportunity to mentally and physically review the next combination. If it is distracting for other groups to perform, then just turn away from the performance taking place, stand quietly, and mentally review the sequence of the next combination. In some classes marking the steps of the current or next combination may be considered discourteous. Instead, train yourself to visualize your performance with correct technique, rhythm, and dynamics to the music as it plays. Your teacher will indicate rules about student expectations and use of marking as part of performance preparation.

Reflecting After the Performance Test

After the performance test, take time to reflect on the combinations and your personal performance. Understanding what you did well can help you build on strengths. Identifying areas that need additional work can give you goals to think about in future classes.

SUMMARY

Learning and performing tap has not only physical challenges but intellectual and mental challenges as well. Understanding the languages of tap and tap steps can create a more sophisticated performance and attitude. In addition, developing an appreciation of rhythmic elements, song structure, and music selection will assist with the ability to accent foot sounds with unique music. Applying techniques, movement principles, and protocols lays the foundation of aesthetics and performance artistry. Discovering how to effectively use the feet as instruments is what beginning tap dance is all about.

To find supplementary materials for this chapter such as learning activities, e-journaling assignments, and web links, visit the web resource at www.HumanKinetics.com/BeginningTapDance1E.

Chapter 5

Tap Dance Steps

Many tap dancers believe tap dance is all about the sound of the feet. Jimmy Slyde, one of the best tap dancers, believed tap dance was about creating pictures with every movement. He stated that he was a visual dancer and when he performed he always had a picture in mind (Asante 2002). When you begin to tap dance what pictures would you like to perform? Viewing videos of some of the great tap dancers can help you visualize what your picture will be as you journey through the wonderful art of tap dance.

Tap dance has its unique vocabulary, skills, and techniques. The ultimate goal of any tap class is for you to improve motor development while learning tap technique. Through tap dance, you can also establish a creative basis to discover the elements of dance or movement concepts.

UNDERSTANDING MOVEMENT

To understand movement, you need to know certain elements, or concepts. These concepts help you gain awareness of how to adapt space, time, force, and flow in the physical environment (Perpich Center for Arts Education 2009). They are explained next.

- **Body awareness** defines how the body moves, body control, weight transfer, and balance (Cone & Cone 2005).
- **Spatial sense** is based on the knowledge that you and everyone occupy space and any movement defines internal body space and general space (Elliott 1997). The quality of your movement is inspired by the elements of direction, level, and range.
- **Direction,** or line of motion, is where you move through space: in a circle, forward, sideways, or backward.
- **Level,** or the transfer of weight from the body's center of gravity, can be performed above center of gravity (high) or below center of gravity (low).
- **Range** is defined by the amount of space the body fills as it moves in pathways either on the floor or in the air (straight, curved, zigzag, spiral, or wavy) (Brehm & Kampfe 1997).
- **Relationship awareness** can include body parts, people, and objects and refers to what and to whom the body relates.
- You can experience the use of **time** through inner rhythms such as breath or pulse or external rhythmic elements such as tempo or speed of movement.
- **Force** of movement is the release or compression of energy, the pull of gravity, and the sensation of heavy or light.
- **Flow** can be sustained movement or a constant flow of smooth energy and percussive movement that ends or changes suddenly and lacks continuity.

You can both verbally and kinesthetically express emotions, ideas, and moods within these elements while exploring fundamental movement and technique (Van't Hof 2002). When you experience dance elements, you can create dance language and movement literacy while understanding and performing tap dance technique (Feldman 1996).

FOOT POSITIONS AND SYMBOLS

Tap dance has five positions of the feet, which are performed at either the barre or the center. In each position, the weight is equally distributed on both feet, the hips are squared to the front, and the legs are either turned out from the hip joints with the feet in classic foot positions or facing front with the feet parallel. Using these positions of the foot (figure 5.1) while performing flaps, shuffles, and toe and heel drops, you will increase strength, balance, and coordination, which will improve your overall tap technique.

First position: Turned out—Heels touch while toes point outward. Parallel—Feet are side by side.

Second position: Turned out—Feet are the same as in first position turned out, except separated approximately shoulder-width apart. Parallel—Feet are the same as in first position parallel, except separated under the shoulders.

Third position: Turned out—The heel of the front foot is touching the middle of the back foot.

Fourth position: Turned out—One foot is in front of other, about one foot length apart. Parallel—One foot is in front of the other.

Fifth position: Turned out—The heel of the front foot is at the toe of the back foot.

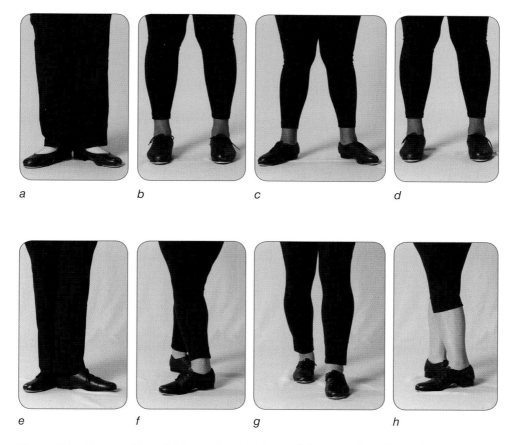

Figure 5.1   First position: (*a*) turned out, (*b*) parallel; second position: (*c*) turned out, (*d*) parallel; (*e*) third position turned out; fourth position: (*f*) turned out, (*g*) parallel; and (*h*) fifth position turned out.

Figure 5.2 shows foot symbols to assist in learning weight and toe–heel changes. Use these when learning basic tap steps and terminology. Foot symbols are used to assist you in distinguishing toe, heel, right foot, and left foot weight exchanges. Most beginners express that this is the most difficult part of learning to tap dance. This visual will assist you in breaking down each tap step and will make learning tap steps easier. Basic tap step terms are included along the most basic movement and steps.

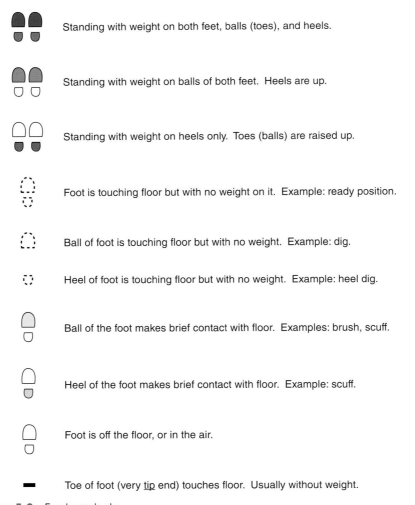

Standing with weight on both feet, balls (toes), and heels.

Standing with weight on balls of both feet. Heels are up.

Standing with weight on heels only. Toes (balls) are raised up.

Foot is touching floor but with no weight on it. Example: ready position.

Ball of foot is touching floor but with no weight. Example: dig.

Heel of foot is touching floor but with no weight. Example: heel dig.

Ball of the foot makes brief contact with floor. Examples: brush, scuff.

Heel of the foot makes brief contact with floor. Example: scuff.

Foot is off the floor, or in the air.

Toe of foot (very tip end) touches floor. Usually without weight.

Figure 5.2 Foot symbols.

▶ LOCOMOTOR MOVEMENTS WITH EVEN RHYTHMS

People use basic locomotor movements in everyday movement, sporting activity, and in dance. These steps are used in combination with other basic tap steps. The following are locomotor movements that have even rhythms, meaning that they are performed slowly or quickly, but not both, throughout. For example, you use an even rhythm when performing a walk with the left foot stepping slowly and the right foot stepping slowly, keeping the rhythm the same throughout.

Walk

A walk is as simple as placing one foot in front of the other, transferring weight from the back foot to the front. In tap, a walk is the same as a step (ball of one foot to ball of the other foot.

Count	Footwork	Cue
1, 2	Start with weight on the right foot and place the left foot forward. Transfer weight from the right foot as soon as you place the left foot.	Step or walk forward

Run

Unlike the walk, the run is an impact step. This means that both feet are in the air at the same time.

Count	Footwork	Cue
1, 2	Start with weight on the right foot. Lift both feet slightly in the air. As you land, transfer the weight from the right (back) foot to the left (forward). Land with the knee bent to reduce the possibility of injury.	Run

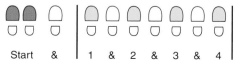

Leap

A leap is similar to a run, except you are suspended in the air longer and higher. Unlike a run, however, both legs are straight. Imagine leaping over a log, springing from one foot to the other.

Count	Footwork	Cue
1, 2	Start with the weight on the right foot, and lift your body up while keeping both legs straight. While the body is suspended, start transferring weight from the back (right) foot forward and land on the left foot. Proper body mechanics involves a plié, or bent knee, when landing on the left foot.	Leap

Hop

When people say that kangaroos hop, they are not correct. Kangaroos do not hop; they actually jump. A true hop starts with your weight on *one* foot as you leave the floor, and you land on the same foot.

Count	Footwork	Cue
1-& or &-1	Start with the weight on the right foot while the left knee is bent and the left foot is off the floor. Bend the right knee and straighten the right knee as you leave the floor. As you land back on the right foot, the right knee should bend to absorb shock.	Hop

Jump

A kangaroo does indeed jump, because a jump starts with weight on *both* feet as you leave the floor, and you land on both feet. Jumps and hops are confused in sports. For example, in basketball a layup does not have a jump; it has a hop, yet most coaches call it a jump. Many people think that a bunny hops, but it actually leaps; it starts with a jump from the back legs and ends up on the front legs.

Count	Footwork	Cue
1-& or &-1	Start with your weight on both feet. Bend both knees, then straighten them as you leave the floor. Land on both feet while both knees bend.	Jump

Assemblé (ah-sahm-BLAY)

This term comes from French and means *to assemble*. Think about assembling both feet as they land on the floor.

Count	Footwork	Cue
&-1, 2	Start with your feet in fifth position with the knees bent in **plié**. While the knees are bent, slide the left leg out while supporting your weight on the right leg. As you leave the floor by springing up with the right leg, you will join both legs together in the air and land on both legs in a plié.	Assemblé

Sissonne (see-SAWN)

This term means *to spring*. It was named after Comte de Sissonne. Sissonne is also a place in Northern France.

Count	Footwork	Cue
&-1	Start with your weight on both feet. Plié, or bend both knees. As you straighten both legs, spring into the air. Land on the left or right leg in plié.	Spring

Start & | 1 & 2 & 3 & 4 |

A leap is similar to a run, except you are suspended in the air longer and higher.

▶ LOCOMOTOR MOVEMENTS WITH UNEVEN RHYTHMS

These locomotor movement steps have uneven rhythms; they use both slow and quick movement.

Gallop

A gallop is similar to a skip, except it is easier and involves an asymmetrical gait. The forward foot remains in front throughout the exercise, while the back foot comes up to meet the front foot. Unlike a skip, though, it never passes. A gallop is also known as a fast gait seen in a horse, where all four legs of the horse are off the ground.

Count	Footwork	Cue
1-& or &-1	Start with your weight on both feet in fourth position parallel (one foot in front). Lift the front foot and step forward, then slide the back foot forward. Weight will be transferred from the front to the back with a small lift.	Step, leap

Skip (Version 1)

Some fitness instructors interchange the term *skipping rope* with *jumping rope*. Neither activity involves skipping. A skip involves a hop and a step or a long step and a hop. There are two versions of skipping: Version 1 starts with a hop, and version 2 starts with a step.

Count	Footwork	Cue
&-1, &-2	Put weight on the right foot and hop, leaving the floor and landing on the right foot. Then step on the left foot and do this movement sequence on the left side.	Hop, step

Skip (Version 2)

This version starts with the weight on both feet.

Count	Footwork	Cue
1-&	Lift the right foot and step forward. Then leave the floor and land on the right foot. Repeat this with a forward step of the left foot.	Step–hop

Slide

The slide step has many meanings. The baseball slide step involves the pitcher lifting the lead foot a few inches rather than using a high knee. The electric slide was—and still is—a popular line dance, and the slide step in aerobic dance involves a fast-paced movement that resembles ice skating. Jimmy Slyde used slides as his trademark. He would jump into the air and as he landed, he would press his heels into the floor as if the floor became covered with ice. Slides are also taught as a loco-motor skill for beginners; this type of slide is addressed here. Similar to a gallop, a slide is an asymmetrical gait consisting of a step–leap–step while moving sideways.

Count	Footwork	Cue
1-& or &-1	Begin with the shoulder, hip, and working leg (right) facing the direction of movement (right). Pick up the working leg (right) and step to the side. Leap from the right leg to the left leg while landing with the left knee bent. When landing, the left leg will replace the right leg to assure that movement will be continued to the right of the room. This movement is also referred to as a step–leap–close.	Step–leap

▶ BASIC DANCE STEPS

These basic steps combine locomotor movement and include both uneven and even rhythms. (Video clips of the grapevine and polka steps are not available on the web resource.)

Foxtrot

In 1914, Henry Fox performed trotting movement to ragtime music in his vaudeville show. Although many experts denied he invented the step, it was nevertheless named after him. Today the foxtrot is used in ballroom dance with partners. Learning the basic steps of the foxtrot is important for beginning tap students.

Count	Footwork	Cue
1-&-2-&	Begin with weight on both feet.	Slow, slow
3-&	Step forward with the right foot (*slow*), then step forward with the left foot (*slow*). Step the right foot out to the side (*quick*) and close with the left foot (*quick*). You may have a variation of these steps; however, slow, slow, quick, quick will always be the rhythm.	Quick, quick

Grapevine

The grapevine has many variations. This example allows you to perform to one side for four counts and then to the other side for four counts.

Count	Footwork	Cue
1, 2, 3, 4	Begin with the weight on both feet. Lift the right foot and step to the right side (*count 1*). Pick up the left foot and cross the left foot either in front of or behind the right (*count 2*). While the feet are crossed, pick up the right foot again and step it to the right (*count 3*). The left foot will move next to the right and dig (*count 4*). A dig step allows the ball of the left foot to touch without placing weight on the left foot. This signals that the left foot is now free to reverse the grapevine to the left.	Side, cross, side, dig

Polka

The polka may not be taught in many tap dance classes, but it is a fun step to learn. It is also a genre of dance music. Many people think that it originated in Poland, but it is Bohemian in origin. The step can be danced in a circle or moving forward.

Count	Footwork	Cue
&-1, &-2	Start with weight on both feet. Transfer the weight to the left foot in preparation to perform a hop. Hop on the left foot and step on the right (*&-1*), then step on the left and then step again on the right (*&-2*).	Hop–step, step–step

Schottische (SHOT-ish)

This is an old round dance similar to the polka.

Count	Footwork	Cue
1, 2, 3, 4	Start with weight on both feet. Step forward on the right foot, step forward on the left foot, step forward on the right again, and then perform a hop from the right foot, landing on the right.	Step, step, step, hop

Triplet

The triplet consists of movement in three steps, which are performed forward, side, or back.

Count	Footwork	Cue
1, 2, 3	Start with weight on both feet. Step any directions with the left foot. Follow this step with a right step and again with a left step.	Step left, step right, step left Run, run, run *or* step, step, step

Two-Step

The two-step has various dance meanings, including the country-western dance called the Texas two-step, the night club dance called the California two-step, or even a break dance acrobatic maneuver. As a beginner, you will learn just a basic two-step move.

Count	Footwork	Cue
1-& 2-& 3-&	Start with the weight on both feet. Step forward with your right foot (*quick*), then with the left foot (*quick*); step forward with your right (*slow*), then with your left (*slow*). You can also perform it as step forward with your right foot and close left behind right, then step forward with the right and then left. Several variations exist, but the rhythm is the same: quick, quick, slow, slow.	Quick, quick Slow Slow

Waltz

Although it is best known in ballroom dance, you can perform the waltz in tap dance. The steps are the same.

Count	Footwork	Cue
1, 2, 3	Start with your weight on both feet. Step the right foot forward, step the left foot to the left side, then close right to left with the weight on the right foot; then begin the sequence again with the left foot, stepping the right foot to the right and closing with the weight on the left foot.	Step, side, close

▶ TAP STEPS WITH ONE SOUND

The following are basic one-sound steps. These steps are the building blocks of other more complicated tap steps. They are presented in order of progression.

Step

A step is a walk. Depending on the style of tap taught, your weight is either on both the ball and heel of the foot or just the ball of the foot. Weight is transferred from one foot to the other.

Count	Footwork	Cue
1, 2 *or* 1-&	Begin with your weight on both feet; your teacher will specify whether the weight needs to be on the balls and heels or just the balls of the feet. Transfer the weight to the left leg, then pick the right foot up and place it in any direction, transferring the weight from the left to the right foot. Repeat this exercise to the other side.	Walk, walk *or* step, step

Dig

A dig is like a step but without the weight transfer. The sound that a dig makes is the same as with a step. You dig with either the ball of the foot or the heel of the foot but not both. This can also be called a toe dig or a heel dig.

Count	Footwork	Cue
1	Start with your weight on both feet. Lift the right foot and touch the ball or the heel on the floor without transferring weight. Usually a dig means that foot is a free foot, or ready for another step.	Dig

Heel

The heel of the tap shoe makes a distinct sound compared with that made with the ball of the shoe. Some teachers call this step a *heel drop*. It could include one or both heels dropping either at the same time or one after the other.

Count	Footwork	Cue
1	Start with your weight on the balls of the feet. Drop the right heel down, transferring weight to the right foot while the heel is hitting the floor. You may also try starting with weight on the balls of the feet and drop both right and left heels down, keeping weight on both feet. Another way to perform a heel is to start with the weight on both feet and pick up the right foot, then tap the heel of the right foot forward or side without transferring weight.	Heel

Toe Tip

Your tap shoes are designed with a small piece of metal on the very tip of the shoe. This adds another type of sound in combination with the ball and heel of the shoe.

Count	Footwork	Cue
1	Start by standing with the weight on both feet. Lift the right foot and hit the very tip of the toe tap on the floor either next to or behind the left foot.	Toe

Toe dig (left), heel dig (middle), and toe tip (right).

Brush

Like the step, a brush is a foundation step from which other more complex steps build. You can perform a brush in all directions: forward, back (also called a *spank*), out to the side, or into the standing leg. A brush involves the ball of the foot making contact with the floor.

Count	Footwork	Cue
1	Start with weight on both feet. Lift the right foot and strike the ball of the foot briefly on the floor while keeping the weight on the left leg. A brush does not have weight transfer and is performed by the ankles, not the knee.	Brush

Chug

The chug is named after the sound it makes. You can perform it using both feet or one foot.

Count	Footwork	Cue
1	For a chug using both feet, start with the weight on the balls of both feet. Slide forward, forcing the heels of both feet down. For the end position, the weight is on both the balls and the heels. For a chug using only one foot, start with all the weight on the ball of the right foot with the heel up. Slide on the ball of the foot forward, forcing the heel of the right foot down to the floor. For the end position, the weight is on both the ball and heel of the right foot.	Chug

Scuff

The scuff is similar to the brush, but you strike the heel tap forward. Think about scuffing up the floor with the heel.

Count	Footwork	Cue
1	Start with the weight on both feet. Lift the right foot and strike the bottom of the right heel tap on the floor. Do not transfer the weight.	Strike

Stamp

A stamp uses the entire foot and includes a weight change.

Count	Footwork	Cue
1	Start with the weight on both feet. Lift the right foot and strike the floor using the entire foot while shifting weight from the left to the right.	Stamp

Stomp

A stomp is like a stamp, but it has no weight transfer.

Count	Footwork	Cue
1	Start with weight on both feet. Lift the right foot and strike the floor with the entire foot and immediately lift the right foot up.	Stomp

▶ TAP STEPS WITH TWO SOUNDS

The following steps all have two sounds and build from the previous steps.

Ball-Change

The ball–change is one of the most used dance steps. With a ball–change you know that there will always be a weight transfer (change) while using the ball of the foot. To perform a ball–change you simply *change feet* on the balls of the feet. You can perform this step in various ways: crossed in back, crossed in front, back to front, apart, or front to back. This step is done with an uneven rhythm.

Count	Footwork	Cue
1-& *or* &-1	A simple ball–change starts with the weight on both feet. Lift the right foot and place just the ball of the foot on the floor in front of the left foot. Transfer the weight from both feet to the right front foot (*ball*). Then, shift the weight back to the left foot (*change*). Now all the weight is on the left foot, and the right foot is ready to perform another step.	Ball–change

Flap

A flap is a combination of a brush and a step. You can perform it to the front, back, or side.

Count	Footwork	Cue
&-1	Start with the weight on both feet. Lift the right foot and strike just the ball of the right foot against the floor (*brush*), then transfer the weight from the left to the right (*step*). In most styles, the heel does not touch the floor.	Brush–step *or* flap

Slap

The slap is like the flap, but it has no weight transfer. Slaps can be performed to the front, side, or back.

Count	Footwork	Cue
&-1	Start with weight on both feet. Lift the right foot and strike just the ball of the right foot against the floor. Keep weight on the left leg; don't transfer the weight.	Brush–toe *or* slap

Shuffle

"Shuffle Off to Buffalo" was a song sang in the 1933 film of the musical *42nd Street*. Shuffles are simple brushes in any direction.

Count	Footwork	Cue
&-1	Start with the weight on both feet. Lift the right foot and brush forward, then back.	Brush–brush *or* shuffle

▶ TAP STEPS WITH THREE SOUNDS

The following steps combine basic steps to create three sounds.

Flap–Heel

The flap–heel combines one brush, one step, and one heel drop. You can perform it forward or back.

Count	Footwork	Cue
&-1, 2	Start with the weight on both feet. Lift the right foot and brush the ball of the foot forward. Step with the ball of the right foot, and transfer the weight from the left foot to the ball of the right foot. With the weight on the ball of the foot, drop the heel and transfer weight to the entire right foot.	Flap–heel

Shuffle–Step

A shuffle–step combines two brushes with one step along with weight transfer.

Count	Footwork	Cue
&-1, 2	Start with the weight on both feet. Lift the right foot and brush forward, then back. Step on the right foot as you transfer weight from the left foot to the right. Most instructors ask you to stay on the ball of the foot when performing a step.	Brush, brush–step *or* shuffle–step

Shuffle–Cross–Step

A shuffle–cross–step is a lead-up step for front Irish steps.

Count	Footwork	Cue
&-1, 2	Start with the weight on both feet. Lift the right foot and brush forward, then brush back across the front of the left foot. Step the right foot in front of the left; end the step with the right foot in front of the left.	Brush–brush–cross–step *or* shuffle–cross–step

Cha-Cha-Cha

This step comes from the cha-cha, a Latin dance that originated in Cuba. It is called a triplet, or a *step–step–step*. You can perform it to the front, side, or back.

Count	Footwork	Cue
1-&-2	Start with the weight on both feet. Step right, step left, then step right.	Step–step–step

Chassé (sha-SAY)

A chassé is like a slide step; it means *to chase*. In square dance, it is called a *sashay*. You can perform this step forward, backward, or to the side.

Count	Footwork	Cue
1, &-2	Start with the weight on both feet. Step to the right, follow with a step of the left foot to replace the right foot (chase), and step again on the right foot.	Step, ball–change

A chassé is a like a slide step.

Riff

The riff is taught in various ways depending on the teacher. Some instructors will teach this step using the toe tip rather than the ball of the foot.

Count	Footwork	Cue
1, &-2	Start with the weight on both feet. Brush the ball of the right foot; while the right foot is off the ground, drop the right heel, leaving the ball of the right foot off the floor. While the weight is still on the left foot, drop the left heel.	Brush, heel, heel

Trenches

Trenches has two variations: one performed to the back and another performed to the side. For beginners, the variation to the back is discussed. Some teachers call this step *falling off the log* or *over the top*. In this version, you leap to the right while dragging the left foot back; the left arm is in front while the right arm is back.

Count	Footwork	Cue
&-1, &-2	Begin with the weight on both feet. Shift the weight to the right foot while scraping or sliding the left foot to the back, and land on the right foot in front. Some teachers teach the left toe tip after the right foot leaps forward.	Scrape, leap *or* scrape, leap–toe

▶ TAP STEPS WITH FOUR OR MORE SOUNDS

The following steps combine basic steps or locomotor movements to produce more complex steps. The names of some of these steps were created by or named after famous tap dancers. These steps appear in alphabetical order.

Buffalo (Single)

The song "Shuffle Off to Buffalo" is responsible for the tap step named buffalo.

Count	Footwork	Cue
1, &-a-2	Start with the weight on both feet. Lift the right leg and place it in front of the left shin. Leap from the left foot to the ball of the right foot (*count 1*). With the weight on the right foot, shuffle with the left foot, leap from the right, and land on the ball of the left foot while the right foot rests in front of the left shin (*&-a-2*).	Leap, shuffle–leap

Buffalo (Double)

Buffalo double is the same as buffalo single, but it begins with a flap and an extra count.

Count	Footwork	Cue
&-1, &-a-2	Start with the weight on both feet. Lift the right leg and place it in front of the left shin. Flap the right foot to the right (*&-1*). With the weight on the right foot, shuffle with the left foot and leap from the right to land on the ball of the left foot while the right foot rests in front of the left shin (*&-a-2*).	Flap, shuffle–leap *or* Buffalo

Cramp Roll

John Bubbles of the dance team Buck and Bubbles has been credited with inventing the cramp roll. This step sounds like a drum roll.

Count	Footwork	Cue
1-&-a-2	Start with the weight on both feet with bent knees. Spring up, leaving the floor while landing with the weight on the ball of the right foot, then the ball of the left foot, followed by a right heel drop, then a left heel drop.	Toe–toe–heel–heel

Essence Soft-Shoe Time Step: Single Front Essence

The term *essence* is associated with the soft-shoe. The soft-shoe was originally performed without metal taps and was made popular in vaudeville acts.

Count	Footwork	Cue
1-&-a-2 3-&-a-4 5-&-a-6 &-a-7 &-a-8	Start with the weight on both feet. Step the right foot to the right (*step*) and brush the left foot across in front of the right (*brush*). Step the ball of the left foot in front of the right foot (*ball*). Lift the right foot in back of the left, and change weight to the right (*change*). Reverse the step to the left side. Repeat it again to the right side; the left foot is free, and you perform a back brush step on the ball of the left foot, lift the right foot, and change weight to the right foot (*change*). Then, brush the left foot again in front of the right while stepping in front of the ball of the right foot (*ball*), and then change weight with the right foot (*change*) and do another back brush with the left foot and ball–change.	Step–brush, ball–change Step–brush, ball–change Step–brush, ball–change Brush–ball–change Brush–ball–change

Essence Soft-Shoe Time Step: Double Front Essence

This step is like the single front essence, but it begins with a flap, making one extra sound.

Count	Footwork	Cue
&-1-&-a-2 &-3-&-a-4 &-5-&-a-6 &-a-7-&-a-8	Start with the weight on both feet. Flap the right foot to the right and brush the left foot across in front of the right. Step the ball of the left foot in front of the right foot (*ball*). Lift the right foot in back of the left and change weight to the right foot (*change*). Reverse the sequence to the left side. Repeat it to the right side; the left foot is free. Perform a back brush step on the ball of the left foot (*ball*), lift the right foot, and change the weight to the right foot (*change*). Then brush the left foot again in front of the right while stepping in front of the right (*ball*), and then change weight with the right foot (*change*) and do another back brush step with the left foot and ball–change.	Flap, brush–ball–change Flap, brush–ball–change Flap, brush–ball–change Brush–ball–change, brush–ball–change

Falling Off the Log

This step has several versions. One involves a grapevine-type step and another is simply dragging the feet back and hitting the toe tips. Some teachers call this step *trenches*. The falling off the log described here is more like a visual of falling off a log.

Count	Footwork	Cue
1, 2, 3, 4	Start with the weight on both feet. Leap the right foot to the right while extending the left leg straight out to the left. While crossing the left leg in front of the right leg, leap on the left foot while extending the right leg back. Leap on the right foot to the right again while extending the left leg out toward the left again. Leap on the left foot to the left while kicking the right leg across in front of the left.	Leap, leap, kick, kick

Flap–Ball–Change

A flap–ball–change combines a brush and a step. You can perform it in any direction.

Count	Footwork	Cue
&-1, &-2	Start with the weight on both feet. Brush the ball of the right foot and step right (*flap*), then step the ball of the left foot behind the right foot (*ball*) and change the weight by stepping the right foot in place (*change*).	Brush–step, step–step *or* flap, ball–change

Going No Place

Going no place is one of many terms for the same step. It refers to the constant replacing of one foot with the other.

Count	Footwork	Cue
1, 2, 3, 4	Begin with the weight on both feet. Step the right foot forward. Cross the left foot over the right foot. Step the right foot to the right, and step the left foot to the left.	Step, cross, step, step

Irish

You can perform this step while moving forward, crossing in the front, or crossing in the back while moving backward.

Count	Footwork	Cue
&-1, &-2	Begin with the weight on both feet. Shuffle to the right with the weight on the left foot, then hop on the left foot and step the right foot, ending with the weight on the right foot.	Shuffle, hop–step

Lindy (Triple)

The lindy is an American social dance that is used in swing tap dance.

Count	Footwork	Cue
1, &-2, 3, 4	Begin with the weight on both feet. Step the right foot to the right (*step*). Step the left foot to the right (*ball*) and then step the right foot to the right (*change*). Lift the left foot and cross it in the back of the right (*ball*), and then step the right foot in place (*change*).	Step, ball–change, ball–change

Mambo Step

"Papa Loves Mambo" was a popular song published in 1954 and recorded by Perry Como. The mambo is a Latin dance invented in Havana. The rhythm is different because it usually starts on count 2.

Count	Footwork	Cue
Hold 1, 2, 3, 4	Begin with the weight on both feet. Brush–step or step the right foot forward starting on count 2. While the weight is on the right foot, lift the left foot in back and brush–step or step back and then brush or step right to left.	Forward, back, step, together

Maxie Ford

This step is named after the tap dancer Maxie Ford, a member of a Vaudeville tap dance team called The Four Fords with brother Edwin and sisters Dora and Mabel Ford.

Count	Footwork	Cue
1-&-2- &-3	Start with the weight on both feet. Leap (*1*) or step on the ball of the right foot. Shuffle (*&-2*) with the left foot while weight is on the right foot, leap (*&*) from the right foot to the ball of the left foot, and toe tip (*3*) on the right foot in the back of the left foot. No weight is transferred from the left foot to the toe tip.	Leap, shuffle, leap, toe tip

Military Cramp Roll

Military cramp roll has many styles and is taught in many different ways. The following step is similar to the regular cramp roll, but it begins with a brush.

Count	Footwork	Cue
&-1-&- a-2	With the weight on both feet, brush the right foot forward and step on the ball of the foot (flap). Step on the ball of the left foot and drop the right heel, then the left heel.	Brush, toe, toe, heel, heel

Paddle Turn

A paddle turn involves turning, so learning to spot is a helpful skill (see the section titled Spotting, later in this chapter). You can perform a paddle turn forward or back. Depending on your teacher and style of tap, a paddle turn can involve just ball–change or flap–ball–change.

Count	Footwork	Cue
1 &-2- &-3, &-4 (steps) *or* &-1, &-a-2- &-a-3 &-a-4 (flaps)	Start with the weight on both feet. You will be turning forward to the right. Step or flap on the right foot to the right while turning to the right. While still turning to the right, step or flap on the ball of the left foot and then change weight to the right foot; repeat two more times. You will make a complete turn.	Step, ball–change, ball–change, ball–change *or* flap, brush, ball–change, brush, ball–change, brush, ball–change

Pivot Turn

A pivot turn is used in many sports, especially in basketball. It allows the player to move from one direction to the other without being penalized for a walking violation. A pivot turn in dance is the same type of move.

Count	Footwork	Cue
1, &-2	Start with the weight on both feet. Step the right foot forward while keeping the weight between both feet in fourth position parallel. While on the balls of both feet, shift your position from front to the left side, then facing back. End the move with the weight on the left foot, still in fourth position parallel.	Step, pivot, turn

Scissors

This is just one variation of the step, which may be called by another name. Peru has a traditional dance called the Scissor, which is a form of break dancing except they use scissors while dancing. Another scissor step that is more advanced is a shuffle on the right foot, then a right toe tip, then a left toe tip, a toe heel on the right foot, and then a stamp on the left foot.

Count	Footwork	Cue
&-1, &-2	Begin with the weight on both feet. Shift the weight to the left while leaping the right foot to the right. Cross and leap the left foot in front of the right. Leap again on the right foot to the right, and end with the left heel to the left.	Leap, cross–heel

Shim Sham

This is the simple variation of the shim sham for beginners.

Count	Footwork	Cue
8-&-1	Start with the weight on both feet. Shuffle right, and step right with the weight on the ball of the foot. Shuffle left, and step left with the weight on the left foot. Shuffle–ball–change with the right foot and shuffle right, stepping with the weight on the ball of the right foot.	Shuffle–step
2-&-3		Shuffle–step
4-&-		Shuffle–ball–change
5-&		
6-&-7		Shuffle–step

Sugars

Sugars are used in many swing dances. You can perform them in any direction.

Count	Footwork	Cue
1, 2, 3, 4	With the weight on both feet, step on the ball of the right foot with the right heel twisted inward while the toes are twisted outward. With the weight on the ball of the right foot, twist the ball of the foot inward while the heel is twisting outward.	Twist, twist

Susie Q

The Susie Q is a dance step used in the lindy hop, known as the *heel twist* or *grind walk*. The song "Doin' the Suzie Q" was popular in the 1930s. Another name for this step is *stick in the mud*.

Count	Footwork	Cue
1, 2, 3, 4	Begin with the weight on both feet. Stamp the right foot across the front of the left foot. Shift the weight to the right heel while fanning the right toe from left to right. End the step with a step on the left foot to the left. Step the left foot to the left as the ball of the right foot rises up, and swing to the right side.	Step, twist

Three-Step Turn

You can perform a three-step turn in any direction.

Count	Footwork	Cue
1	Begin with the weight on both feet. Step right while facing right, and step the left foot across to the right. Complete the turn by stepping the right foot facing the same direction you started. This move involves one complete turn with three steps.	Step
2		Step
3, hold 4		Step

Single Time Step—Buck Time Step

Time steps form the foundation of tap dance, and many variations exist. They have been around as long as tap dance itself. A single time step involves a step that has only one (single) sound.

Count	Footwork	Cue
8, 1, &-a-2, &-3	Begin with the weight on both feet. Shift the weight to the left, and stomp right (*8*). Hop (*1*) on the left foot, and shuffle (*&-a*)–step right (*2*), step left (*&*), and step right (*3*).	Stomp, hop, shuffle–step, step–step

Double Time Step

A double time step involves a flap, which gives the step two sounds.

Count	Footwork	Cue
8, 1, &-a-2, &-a-3	Begin with the weight on both feet. Shift the weight to the left and stomp right. Hop on the left foot and shuffle–step to the right, brush–step left, and step right.	Stomp, hop– shuffle–step, flap–step

Triple Time Step

A triple time step involves a shuffle step for three counts.

Count	Footwork	Cue
8, 1, &-a-2, &-a-3, &	Begin with the weight on both feet. Shift the weight to the left and stomp right. Hop on the left foot and shuffle–step right, shuffle–step left, and step right.	Stomp, hop– shuffle–step, shuffle–step, step

Waltz Clog Time Step Single

The waltz clog time step is as simple as a step–shuffle–ball–change. Some teachers teach the step beginning with a leap; others teach the shuffle performed across the supported foot as with the Irish. The main thing to remember is to step in the direction you want to travel.

Count	Footwork	Cue
1	Begin with the weight on both feet. Step and leap with the right foot to the right. Shuffle (brush–brush) with the left foot still facing stage right, then step the ball of the left foot behind the right. Change the weight from the left foot to the right foot.	Leap *or* step
&-2		Shuffle
&-3		Ball–change
	Another way to perform this step involves crossing the left foot as you shuffle, performing the ball in front of the right foot and the change behind the left foot.	

▶ OTHER STEPS

The following steps combined with other tap steps can add style and finesse to any combination. These steps or movements usually involve little to no sound.

Knee Bounces

Knee bounces are used in combination with other steps for an added flair. Knee bounces do not create sound.

Count	Footwork	Cue
1, 2 *or* 1-&	With the weight on both feet, bend both knees and straighten them, moving down and up.	Bounce, bounce

Knee Pops

Knee pops can add style. They are commonly used in the **legomania** style of dance.

Count	Footwork	Cue
1-&-2-&	With the weight on both feet, lift the heels up as the body contracts forward, then quickly drop the heels down.	And pop, and pop

Lunge

You can add a lunge at the beginning of, during, or at the end of any tap combination. You can make a sound with a lunge if you incorporate a step either before or after it.

Count	Footwork	Cue
1 *or* &-1	With the weight on both feet, step in any direction with a bent knee while the other leg is straight.	Lunge

Passé

Passé means to pass. Think of it as passing your foot up your leg.

Count	Footwork	Cue
&-1	Begin with the weight on both feet. Slide the right foot up the left leg to the inside of the knee while pointing the toes. You can perform this movement with the feet turned out or parallel.	Passé

Pencil Turn

A pencil turn is taught many different ways. It can have a nice dragging sound to add to any combination.

Count	Footwork	Cue
1 & 2	Start with the weight on both legs. Using your spotting technique while turning (see Spotting, later in this chapter), step the right foot and turn clockwise while dragging the toes of the left foot behind the right as it follows the turn. You can also perform the pencil turn while turning backward: Step the right foot and turn counterclockwise by leading with the left foot, dragging as you turn.	Step, drag, turn

Shimmy

A shimmy is performed with many steps. It only involves the shoulders moving in opposition of each other.

Count	Footwork	Cue
&-1 &-2	No footwork is involved in this move. Start with the shoulders relaxed. Press the right shoulder forward with the arm down while pressing the left shoulder back with the arm down. Reverse. Start slowly, then pick up the pace.	Shimmy

Spin

A spin involves a turn with weight being either on both heels, both toes, or whole feet. You can also perform it on one foot.

Count	Footwork	Cue
&-1, 2	One-foot turn: With the weight on both feet, step the right foot to the right and spin on the right foot. Two-foot turn: With weight on both feet, step the right foot to the right and quickly place the left foot next to the right while turning.	Spin, spin

Spotting

Spotting is a technique using the head and focus of eyes to prevent becoming dizzy while turning. Spotting creates a constant orientation of where you are in the studio or on stage. The head rotates much faster than the body during the turn and stops to fix the gaze on a location on the walls or an object in the studio.

Count	Footwork	Cue
&-1, &-2	Footwork can involve any type of turn. Focus your eyes on a location in the room. While turning, keep your eyes focused on that location until you need to turn the head. Turn the head very quickly to refocus on that location.	Look–whip, look–whip

Sway

A sway is a simple step of shifting the weight quickly from right to left or reverse.

Count	Footwork	Cue
&-1, 2	Begin with the weight on both feet. Shift the weight to the right foot either by stepping on the right foot to the right or just bending the right knee without lifting the foot.	Sway, sway

SUMMARY

This chapter introduced dance elements along with a progression of basic tap dance steps. All tap steps build from either locomotor movements or basic one-sound steps. When learning the more complex steps, always review the basics. Tap incorporates not only steps but also proper counts and rhythm. It is best to start with basic steps with correct counts or rhythm before attempting the more complicated steps.

To find supplementary materials for this chapter such as video clips of tap steps, learning activities, e-journaling assignments, and web links, visit the web resource at www.HumanKinetics.com/BeginningTapDance1E.

Chapter 6

Developing Tap Technique

Tap dance is a physical activity that is also an art form. Each tap class requires physical exertion, concentration, patience, and commitment. Tap dance is also a fun, feel-good, noisy activity; with practice, you can use it to express yourself through performing simple combinations with correct form and sound. With time and attention, you can progress to more complex movements. It is an activity that provides you immediate feedback; you know quickly whether what you are doing is correct or not. Tap is not just about performing the physical steps correctly but also about correctly keeping with the sound and rhythm. Although tap dance does not demand some of the extreme movements that you see in other dance forms, it still requires a logical class structure that allows you to learn and develop correct technique and provides a safe way to progress as a dancer. This structure begins with proper preparation and warm-up. Depending on styles and individual preferences, teachers structure their classes in their own ways. This chapter provides a sample class structure that may differ from that of your teacher.

PRE–WARM-UP

Pre–warm-up exercises are activities you do to prepare your body for the class warm-up. They depend on your age, your ability, and your present condition or history of injury. These exercises can be as simple as a brisk 5-minute walk or some light stretches. Your teacher may suggest specific exercises, or you may perform pre–warm-up activities that you have done for other physical activities. Pre–warm-up activities can include the following:

◆ While holding on to a chair, barre, or wall, perform toe–heel flexes and extensions to wake up the feet; flex and extend the feet 10 times each.

◆ Perform 10 straight-leg heel raises (relevés).

◆ While still holding onto the barre, chair, or wall, lift one knee up to the chest or waist and hold it for 3 to 5 seconds. Lower the leg down and bring up the other knee. Perform this exercise 4 times.

◆ Perform 10 squats or knee bends.

WARM-UP

A warm-up prepares the body for the workout. It needs to elevate the body temperature and be specific to the activity of the class. Although some dance teachers have used the warm-up part of the class to perform intense stretching, it is not recommended because muscles must be properly warmed up to allow for safe stretching. After the warm-up, which usually lasts around 5 to 7 minutes, you should feel your body become warmer but not to the point that you are sweating profusely. Warm-up is usually performed in bare feet. Some students feel uncomfortable walking in public without foot covers; if this is the case, wear nonslip socks. Warm-up activities can include the following:

◆ Walk across the floor to the beat of the music; repeat backward.

◆ Walk across the floor on the balls of the feet; repeat backward.

◆ Perform toe–heel across the floor; repeat backward.

◆ Perform heel–toe across the floor; repeat backward.

◆ Skip across the floor; repeat backward.

◆ Perform any other basic locomotor movements across the floor.

Isolations are usually part of the warm-up. Although they are associated more with jazz and modern dance, they are beneficial to you as a beginning tap student. Isolation exercises train you to understand how your body moves in various directions, thus improving coordination. These exercises can be performed either before or after locomotor movements. Isolation exercises are performed in the center and include the following:

- **Neck:** Stand with the weight equally between both legs. Rotate the head to look right and then left four times. With the shoulders square and torso upright, look straight down, then straight ahead, and then up four times.
- **Shoulders:** Roll both shoulders backward and forward four times. Roll the right shoulder forward while the left rolls back four times, and then reverse.
- **Rib cage:** Without moving the shoulders and the hips, do the following:
  - Move just the rib cage to the right and then left four times.
  - Move just the rib cage to the front and then back four times.
  - Move just the rib cage in a circle: right; to the back; to the left; to the front, four times; then reverse it.
- **Hips/Pelvis:** Without moving the rest of the body, do the following:
  - Shift the weight to the right leg and stick the right hip out; bounce four times, then reverse to the left.
  - Shift the weight to the right leg and circle the hips around four times, then reverse to the other side.
  - Circle the pelvis around without engaging the upper body or legs.
  - Move the pelvis to the front, then back; think about pushing the hips (front) then pulling the hips (back).
- **Legs:** With the weight on the right leg, roll the left leg into the midline of the body then back out four times; reverse the movement. With the right leg rotating toward the midline, place the heel on the floor and then bend the knee. Repeat the movement four times, then switch sides.
- **Ankles and feet:** With the weight on the left foot, circle the right foot clockwise while moving the leg to the front, the side, and back. Reverse the foot circle counterclockwise starting with the leg in the back, side, and then front; repeat on the other side. Then, with the weight on the left foot, point and flex the right foot while moving the leg to the front, side, and back; reverse back, side, and front. Repeat on the other side.

AT THE BARRE

The barre can be used to develop tap techniques thanks to legendary tap instructor Al Gilbert. Gilbert developed over 1,000 graded dances for teachers and students (Rowan 2003), mostly taught as barre exercises. Not all tap teachers use the barre during class, but doing so has many benefits for improving technique and balance. The barre workout in this chapter emphasizes proper posture, form, technique, and precision. It will assist you in gaining a good sense of line through the legs, torso, arms, and head.

The use of the barre improves balance, especially for beginning dancers. Balance involves your center of gravity over your legs, which function as your base of

TECHNIQUE TIP ▶▶▶▶▶▶▶▶▶▶

During the barre exercises, keep your head up and look forward. Beginning dancers naturally tend to look toward the feet. Although it is understandable—most of the action is at your feet—you should avoid the habit of looking down. It not only is aesthetically unappealing and uses poor alignment, but it is also unnecessary; your body has the ability to transmit a sense of position without the need to look.

support. When standing, it is easier to balance with your legs wide apart because you are using a wider base of support. In tap dance, you must be able to balance over one leg and even on the ball of the foot on that one leg. This may be problematic for beginners. Vision, vestibular (inner ear) sense, and proprioceptive sense also contribute to balance. Proprioceptors send and receive impulses to the nervous system regarding the position of all body parts during a movement. The more you train these proprioceptors, the better your balance is; barre exercises assist with this type of training.

Etiquette at the Barre

Following proper etiquette at the barre keeps the class safe and orderly. When you stand at the barre, you usually perform exercises with the right leg first, and when you switch sides, you always turn toward the barre.

Stand with the left side to the barre so that the right foot is further from the barre; the right foot is considered the working foot while weight is on the left. Stand erect with the left hand lightly placed on the barre a little further forward of the body. Place the right arm out to the side or place the hand or fist on the hip (see figure 6.1). Changing to the other side typically begins on count 5 with the

Figure 6.1   Correct position at the barre.

ball of the working foot in back of the standing foot, followed by a *change* on count 6. Count 7 is a turn with the weight on the barre-side foot turning in toward the barre and stepping. On count 8 you now have a new *barre-side* foot, which means a new working foot.

Sample Barre Exercises

Barre exercises usually start with something as simple as nerve taps. Nerve taps are performed using the working foot with the heel almost touching the floor while the ball of the foot is tapping as fast as possible. These taps are performed to the front, side, back, and side again, finishing with a ball–change (step–step) turn to the other side. This step engages the anterior tibialis (shin) and is a great way to warm up the lower leg.

Next, do a simple brush with one sound, performing four to eight brushes to the front, the side, and the back. Barre exercises progress with simple variations. For example, return to the first side and perform the brushes again for four counts to each side, then add a ball–change, then turn to the other side and repeat the exercise with the other leg. Other barre exercises include steps with one sound such as heels, scuffs, and stamps along with steps with two sounds such as shuffles and flaps.

Barre exercises assist in the learning process of building more complex steps from simple ones using one or two sounds with the added benefit of using the barre for balance. The more you work on barre exercises, the more you develop balancing skills that will train you to better perform these skills later without the use of the barre. Another important use of the barre is to work on very complex steps with jumps and leaps. The barre can assist in proper landing techniques for safety and clarity.

> ## ACTIVITY ▶ ▶ ▶ ▶ ▶ ▶ ▶ ▶ ▶ ▶ ▶
>
> ### Practicing Alignment Outside of Class
>
> Proper alignment must be practiced throughout the day and not just in dance class. Find a friend that will correct you if she catches you slumping or rolling your shoulders too far forward. Think about drawing a straight line from your ear lobes to your shoulders, down through your waist, knees, ankles, and the arch of the foot. Check your alignment throughout the day until you train yourself to adjust when needed.

ACROSS THE FLOOR

Although barre exercises have many benefits, they can limit mobility. Taking the steps practiced during the barre exercises and adding locomotor movement help you create more balance and coordination. It also provides you with space to freely move; for most students, it is the favorite part of the class. Usually the steps practiced across the floor are steps that need review. In fact, because there is a limit in your ability to learn new steps in every class, most of the class focuses on reviewing steps previously learned. These well-practiced steps assist in the learning of new steps. During learning, the brain always tries to build on past knowledge or experience. The more movement experience you have, the more the brain can learn.

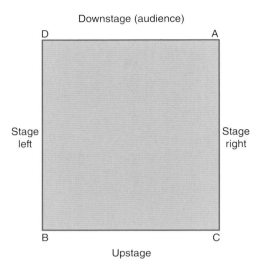

Downstage (audience)

D   A

Stage left   Stage right

B   C

Upstage

Figure 6.2 Stage directions.

Depending on the space, teachers usually have students perform steps from one corner to the opposite corner. For your spatial orientation and for your safety, you should learn stage directions (figure 6.2) before moving across the floor or performing center floor exercises. When performing across-the-floor exercises, start downstage right (*A*) and perform steps toward upstage left (*B*). Then walk from upstage left (*B*) to upstage right (*C*). Then move from upstage right (*C*) to downstage left (*D*). Usually, you move with a small group of about five dancers across the floor and complete the exercise across the floor.

Simple steps across the floor include running flaps, shuffle–steps, shuffle–hop–cross–steps, and flap–ball–changes. Usually any step performed across the floor is performed backward as well. Other combinations include types of turns or steps to the right side and the left side. These simple combinations across the floor work on basic techniques introduced at the barre. It is also a great time to review any steps taught in previous classes.

CENTER FLOOR

The center floor work is the climax of the class. Dance combinations and new tap skills are taught, reviewed, and performed. Depending on the space, you may be facing mirrors, and you and your classmates stand in straight lines. Although beginners tend to avoid the front row, that is the best place to view the instructor, especially if you are shorter than most students. Your teacher stands downstage center while teaching or reviewing steps. When your teacher introduces a new step, stop talking and moving during the visual or verbal instructions. It is hard to see and hear when students are tapping or talking while the teacher is teaching. Once the teacher asks you to practice a new step, then try it. Remember, this is your chance to transfer visual and language cues to your kinesthetic sense; now, you can learn by doing. Dancing in front of the class can be scary and intimidating, but your teacher, who is there to help you, is the only person that is watching you dance. The other students in the class are focused on what they are doing, not what you are doing.

You usually have a couple of minutes to practice new combinations on your own. Some students work in small groups; others prefer working alone. You will find what works best for you. If you have questions, it is tempting to ask for immediate help from your teacher. However, wait until the time the teacher has designated for answering questions or talk to your teacher after class. Teachers have the difficult task of making sure their instructions do not go too slow and bore the class or too fast and frustrate the class. You may be a faster learner compared with others or you may struggle with most steps; either way, be patient and remember that everyone in the class has individual needs. Your needs will be addressed eventually. The teacher may allow you to work with a partner or assign you to work in groups on difficult steps that you may have learned or need help learning.

COOL-DOWN

The cool-down is as important as the warm-up. Depending on the intensity of center floor work, the cool-down should last for around 5 minutes. The cool-down brings your heart rate down to normal and is the perfect time to perform stretches. Lactic acid buildup in the muscles can create soreness from slight to severe; stretching is the best way to limit the severity of this soreness, called delayed-onset muscle soreness. Many dancers only stretch the legs, but this is a mistake; you should stretch all major muscles for optimal health and range of motion. To improve flexibility (increase range of motion) you should perform a long, sustained stretch (static stretch). Stretches that involve bouncing (ballistic stretches) may trigger the stretch reflex, which causes the muscles to contract rather than stretch, which increases the potential for muscle tears. You should only take a stretch to the point of mild tension, not to pain, and hold it for 15 to 30 seconds. Remember to breathe while stretching; it helps relax the muscles even more and also helps with the slight discomfort you may experience when beginning to stretch. Figure 6.3 shows stretching exercises performed in tap class.

a *b*

(continued)

Figure 6.3 Stretches performed in tap class: (*a*) neck; (*b*) shoulders

Figure 6.3 *(continued)* (*c*) triceps; (*d*) biceps; (*e*) chest; (*f*) back; (*g*) sides; (*h*) hamstrings

i

j

k

Figure 6.3   *(continued)* (*i*) inner thighs; (*j*) shins; (*k*) calves.

SUMMARY

This chapter introduced you to the structure or outline of the tap class from pre–warm-up to cool-down. Every teacher teaches tap differently and may or may not use some or all of the examples given in this chapter. Every component of the tap class explained in this chapter helps you to build from basic steps with one sound to more complex steps and combinations. The more you practice the basic steps in class and outside of class, the easier the combinations become.

To find supplementary materials for this chapter such as learning activities, e-journaling assignments, and web links, visit the web resource at www.HumanKinetics.com/BeginningTapDance1E.

Chapter 7

History of Tap Dance

The creation of tap dance is generally credited to African Americans. A look back into the global history of dance proves that although African Americans were responsible for the popularity of what is known as tap dance today, its rich history actually goes back thousands of years. Many groups, nations, and cultures contributed to the formation of tap dance, and throughout the centuries many styles evolved. Today, all age groups enjoy tap dance as a performing art in concert and in musical theater, as a recreational activity, as an academic course in schools and universities, and in other venues.

This chapter demonstrates that the uniqueness of tap dance is directly related to the diverse ethnic groups that contributed to its current form. This chapter leads you through the long journey of tap's creation from the Irish jig and the English hornpipe to the stepping of African and Native American dance. Understanding its history can help you better enjoy and connect with this unique form of physical activity and expressive art.

IRISH DANCE

Over 2,000 years ago, the Celts introduced a unique style of folk dance to Ireland. These ring or circle dances were performed as religious rituals to honor their gods. By the 15th century, Irish dance evolved into foot tapping, low stepping, and high leaps (Knowles 2002). By the mid-16th century, the Irish hey (which evolved into today's *reel*) was presented to the court of Queen Elizabeth. The jig, which means *to jump,* has its origin in England and was performed in the Elizabethan court (Knowles 2002). **William Kemp**, one of the most famous jig performers (1600), was best known as Peter in the play, *Romeo and Juliet* (Collier 1853). He concluded each performance with a jig, which was known as Kemp's Jigge (Knowles 2002).

The popularity of Irish dance by the 18th century was credited to the dancing masters. These Irish dance teachers traveled to local villages teaching dance to peasants (Knowles 2002). By the 1840s, one third of Ireland's population was totally dependent on potatoes as their food source. During this time, a potato blight caused the Great Famine, and one million people died while many others fled to the United States (Oxford 1996). The dancing masters fled as well, and most ended up in New York. The jig, which came with these immigrants, was soon mixed with other cultures, including freed African American slaves in Five Points, a slum in New York (Alan 2007).

ENGLISH STEP DANCE

Clog dancing, or English step dance, has its origin among female mill workers who emulated the sound of the cotton looms with their clogs. Clogs were wooden-soled shoes worn to protect the feet of miners and mill workers. During breaks, workers would dance the reel and jig. Jig contests determined who could make the most sounds with their clogs. One famous clog dancer, **Charlie Chaplin**, performed in a clog troupe called Seven Lancashire Lads in 1897 (Tracey 1993).

Two other types of English dances were the hornpipe and the morris dance. The hornpipe, named after a bagpipe instrument, mimics activities performed by sailors. Captain Hook required his sailors to perform the sailor's hornpipe to prevent boredom and to keep his sailors healthy on ships out to sea (Inglehearn 1993). The morris dance was traditionally performed as a pagan ritual by men, who blackened their faces (Knowles 2002). The blackened faces may have represented masks, a connection to coal mining, or the dark complexion of the Moors (Knowles 2002). Blackened faces were also found in 19th-century American minstrel shows. The morris dance was similar to the African American patting juba (described further in the next section); dancers would rhythmically strike small wooden discs and bells with the hands and knees (Knowles 2002).

AFRICAN DANCE

In many African cultures, dance is an integral part of life. Dance became a form of self-expression, identity, and communication, especially in West Africa. The drumming rhythm closely resembled the pitch of speech (Hill & Sommer 2006).

The use of drums in a Morse code–like fashion allowed communication between tribes. Dance provided entertainment as well as an oral history practice. African drums layered multiple rhythms on top of each other, and dancers moved to each drum using different body parts (shoulders, arms, pelvis, legs, and chest). Each body part moved to the layered rhythms, creating a unique dance style. Hip hop, the robot, and the lindy hop can be traced back to African dance. Several aspects of African dance gave rise to tap dance, including the flatfooted, gliding, shuffling, and dragging steps along with the syncopated musical accent that fell on the second and fourth beat (offbeat) (Hill & Sommer 2006).

During the 1500s, African slaves were brought to North and South America and the Caribbean. African slaves taken to South America and the Caribbean were allowed to continue many of their dance traditions (Knowles 2002). The three most popular dances were the calenda, the chica, and the juba. The calenda was performed by couples and involved pelvic thrusts, thigh patting, jumps, and turns. It was very popular among African slaves and was banned by slave owners for having lewd movements. The Cuban rumba is considered to be a descendant of the calenda dance (Knowles 2002). The chica was also a couple's dance that included hip rotation with an immobile upper body. The juba was a competition dance performed flatfooted and involved upper body movement. Later, when slaps and claps were added as accompaniment, it was called patting juba.

The Stono Rebellion, the largest slave rebellion, took place on September 9, 1739, in South Carolina (Wood 2006). In response to this rebellion, South Carolina

African dance is an integral part of African cultures. It is a form of self-expression, identity, and communication.

established the Negro Act of 1740, which banned slaves from assembling in groups, raising food, earning money, and learning to read English (Wood 2006). It was believed that dancing and drums were important communication devices that plotted the details of the revolt, and slaves were banned from beating drums or blowing horns. This ban on drums gave rise to the use of the rhythmic sounds of body slaps, foot stomps, shuffles, heel beats, and toe beats.

In 1807, international slave trade was banned and American slave owners sold some of their slaves to other plantations (Benton 2011). This further mixed dance styles of different African tribes along with European dance styles. Slave owners considered slaves that could dance more valuable and demanded that they dance while being sold. Slaves performed the buck dance, the pigeon wing, the patting juba, and the cakewalk as a source of entertainment for slave masters and their families (Knowles 2002). Slave owners grouped all African dance styles into one category called *jig* and had slaves compete in jigging contests with other plantation slaves (Knowles 2002).

NATIVE AMERICAN DANCE

Before the European introduction of African slavery, some Native American tribes used war captives from other tribes as slaves (Gallay 2003). When the British settled in the Southern Colonies, some tribes would sell these slaves. Native Americans were enslaved by whites, which transformed Native American tribal relations (Gallay 2003). Before 1720, some Southern Colonies had more Native American slaves than African slaves. Many African slaves escaped and lived with the Native Americans. Native American slave trade ended by 1750 because of the Indian Wars and the growing availability of African slaves. During this transitional period, Africans and Native Americans shared communal quarters along with many customs (Donald 1977).

Native American dancing in North America dates back to prehistoric times (Bingaman 2011). Much like the African Americans, dance was important in the daily lives of the Native Americans. Many of these dances still exist today, and unlike the polyrhythmic beats of African dance, Native American music has a steady 2/4 beat and dancers perform to both vocal and instrumental music. Dance forms vary with tribes; styles are restrained and close to the ground, with very little acrobatics or leaps.

The Cherokee stomp dance incorporates shuffles and stomps and is a follow-the-leader improvisatory style of dance that is affiliated with the green corn ceremony (Cherokee stomp dance, n.d.). No two stomp dances are the same in choreography or beats, and the order of the dancers is male–female in a continuous circle. Several hundred people might participate in this worship dance at one time. It is similar to the ancient running dance.

Ghost dance is a circle dance that came out of a Native American spiritual movement driven by horrible conditions on reservations in the late 1880s. The ghost dance movement was believed to have contributed to the Wounded Knee Massacre in 1890 when the U.S. Army killed at least 153 Lakota Sioux (Liggett 1998). The Bureau of Indian Affairs feared that violence would result from this style of dance, and in 1904 the U.S. government banned some Native American religious practices; it targeted the ghost and sun dance, a ceremony that included dancers being ritually pierced. This ban was not lifted until 1978, when Congress passed the American Indian Religious Freedom Act (Liggett 1998).

MINSTREL SHOWS

The war of 1812 brought a sense of pride and identity to Americans. Society wanted to see their culture explained through entertainment. By the 1840s, minstrelsy, or minstrel shows, were the most popular form of entertainment (Toll 2006). These shows were performed by white men in black face paint (*blackface minstrelsy*) and depicted the white man's stereotype of the African American population. Although white performers have portrayed African Americans as early as the 1600s and in other countries, none were as popular as the famous **Thomas Dartmouth "Daddy" Rice's** performance of Jim Crow. Legend has it that Jim Crow was a crippled slave stable man who was observed by Rice. Rice developed his song and dance routine of this exaggerated, highly stereotyped African American character and went on to be known as the *father of American minstrelsy*. Rice's style of dance consisted of shuffling, limping, and jigging movements. Soon several other acts copied his character, and in 1843 four white men from New York performed as the Virginia Minstrels incorporating violins, castanets, banjos, bones, and tambourines into their act. The Christy Minstrels toured in 1845, introducing the traditional seating of the blackface minstrelsy performers in a semicircle on stage; the tambourine player, *Mr. Tambo,* at one end, the bones player, *Mr. Bones,* at the other, and *Mr. Interlocutor* in the middle (Toll 2006). Unfortunately, these performances depicted African Americans as lazy and stupid and the term *Jim Crow* soon became a racial slur. The famous P.T. Barnum was a producer and promoter of blackface minstrelsy.

After the Civil War, most states in the South passed anti–African American legislation, known as Jim Crow laws (Yenerall 2009). These laws kept African Americans from reaching equality with other Americans and were overruled by the 1954 Supreme Court ruling of Brown v. Board of Education, the 1964 Civil-Rights Act, and the Voting Rights Act of 1965 (Litwack 2006). The popularity minstrels had for over 50 years would soon be replaced with vaudeville, movies, and radio.

DID YOU KNOW? ▶▶▶▶▶▶▶▶

White performers in minstrels were soon replaced by African American performers, who continued to blacken their faces. One of the first African American performers to perform in front of a white audience was **William Henry Lane** ("Master Juba"), who began his career in Manhattan's Five Points neighborhood (Knowles 2002). Five Points was a slum where Irish immigrants and free black people lived and regularly danced together.

VAUDEVILLE

After the Civil War, white-collar workers demanded more entertainment to fill their increased leisure time. Entertainment was divided into classes, and most forms were not appropriate for women and children. A new form of entertainment was needed for a wider audience while maintaining a clean, wholesome atmosphere for families.

In his book *Tap Roots,* Knowles (2002) suggested that Tony Pastor, a former ringmaster with the circus, started what is known as vaudeville in New York in 1881 at the 14th Street Theatre in Tammany Hall. Other scholars credit Benjamin Franklin Keith as the father of vaudeville. Both men wanted to create entertainment that would be clean enough to draw women and children. Vaudeville was open

American vaudeville performers Rosy (1892-1970) and Jenny (1892-1941) Dolly, known professionally as the Dolly Sisters.

to anyone who could entertain, and it was a lucrative career. Comprised mainly of singers and dancers, vaudeville gave rise to other specialty acts such as stunt performers, magicians, high divers, and strong men.

During the peak of vaudeville, tap dance developed into the form that is recognized today. Buck and wing, or clog style, along with the song and dance style of soft-shoe, grew in popularity and included solo, duet, and team performers (Knowles 2002). Metal and jingle taps were created to add more audio effect. It also gave rise to family and children acts, which developed into tandem acts, staged for twins or siblings using shadowing and mirroring techniques. More competition between African American troupes developed, and it included eccentric and acrobatic movements (Knowles 2002).

MOTION PICTURES

Many inventors are responsible for the creation of motion pictures. These short clips were part of an important form of entertainment and were regularly incorporated into shows in the 1900s. This shift of entertainment from live shows to cinema presentations in the 1920s has been considered the cause of the gradual death of vaudeville. In 1923, inventor Lee de Forest premiered several short vaudeville film acts at the Rivoli Theatre in New York City (Adams 2011). In 1927, Warner Brothers released *The Jazz Singer*, a partial sound and silent musical movie. In 1929, MGM released the first all talking, singing, and dancing film *The Broadway Melody*. The film won an Academy Award for Best Picture, which was followed by more successful musical feature films (Kenrick 2011). Although many vaudeville entertainers simply left the stage for the movie industry, tap dance gained even more popularity. Screen musicals were very popular, but they required a great deal of time and resources to create. This proved to be problematic during the economic hard times of the 1930s. During the Great Depression, Hollywood's financial state reduced the creation of musicals. However, in 1933, Warner Brothers released *42nd Street*, a musical that earned millions. Busby Berkeley was given credit for the movie's success because of his choreography, camera work, and staging style (Kenrick 2011).

Movie styles of the 1940s were more patriotic and morale boosting during and after World War II (Kenrick 2011). However, in the 1950s another form of entertainment offered fierce competition to the movie industry; it was television. Movie goers decreased in numbers, and the movie industry created lower-budget movies. Experts say that in spite of this decrease, some of the greatest musical movies were still developed in the 1950s: *An American in Paris* (1951), *Singin' in the Rain* (1952), and *Seven Brides for Seven Brothers* (1957; Frank 1994).

The 1960s brought great movies such as *Mary Poppins* (1964), *The Sound of Music* (1965), *West Side Story* (1961), *Funny Girl* (1968), and *Oliver!* (1968; Kenrick 2011).

The 1970s had many bad movies; however, some did shine. Well-known movies such as *Jesus Christ Superstar* (1973), the Who's *Tommy* (1975), *Sgt. Pepper's Lonely Hearts Club Band* (1978), *The Rose* (1979), *Grease* (1978), and *The Rocky Horror Picture Show* (1975) had their own cult followings.

By the 1980s, experts say that musical movies were dead and that several produced in that time period proved that point (Kenrick 2011). However, musical films such as *The Little Mermaid* (1989) and *Little Shop of Horrors* (1986) brought back the craze for musical movies. The 1990s again brought Disney to the forefront with musical movies such as *Beauty and the Beast* (1991), *Aladdin* (1992), *The Lion King* (1994), and *Pocahontas* (1995).

In 2000, remakes of popular musicals made into film, such as *Chicago* (2002), *Phantom of the Opera* (2005), and *Rent* (2005), did not spark interest. However, in 2006, it would take a small nonsinging penguin to revive interest in tap dancing. This animated film *Happy Feet* (2006) won the Academy Award for Best Animated Feature.

Although the history of tap dance covers thousands of years and involves the contributions of many cultures for development, each contribution made tap what it is today; it is always evolving. For every generation that enjoys what the past has created, the future will continue. Through the lives of the stars of tap dance, we can learn the more human side of this great dance form.

ARTISTS OF TAP DANCE

Many names are associated with tap dance; each dancer has a story to tell. All famous tap dancers have borrowed from other dancers who came before them, and together they made tap what it is today. This section provides a brief summary of tap dance artists; those mentioned are in no way more important than those not mentioned.

With the invention of the radio and talking pictures, people of the early 1900s found unique sources of entertainment. A boom in music and dance provided the opportunity to produce some great tap dancers. **King Rastus Brown** was considered one of the greatest buck dancers in the New York area in 1903 (Frank 1994). He rarely performed for a white audience, thus keeping him from fame. Experts say that he even created the time step (Frank 1994). **Willie Covan** started dancing at the age of 5, and in his teens he performed with his future wife, brother, and a friend to form a group called the Four Covans (1933). Willie Covan performed in minstrel shows and is accredited with creating the rhythm waltz clog (Frank 1994).

Ruby Keeler is considered the first tap dancing star of the silver screen and performed in the popular movie *42nd Street* (1933). Keeler, a buck dancer, incorporated ballet and jazz movement in her performances (Hill 2010). **Peg Leg Bates** (1930s) redefined tap dance as the most famous one-legged dancer ever. His artificial leg, or peg, was half rubber and half leather, which made a unique sound and intense rhythms as he performed (Frank 1994). **Leonard Reed** and **Willie Bryant** (1930s), of the famous Shim Sham Shimmy dance routine, performed a heel-and-toe combination danced to four eight-bar choruses (Frank 1994).

The Cotton Club, a famous night spot located in Harlem during Prohibition, was owned by gangsters in the 1920s. It was limited to African American performers who performed to a white-only audience and produced some of the greatest tap stars. Two brothers, the famous **Nicholas Brothers**, first hired for the radio show *The Horn and Hardart Kiddie Hour,* debuted their high leaps, springs, flips, and fast-

American tap dancing duo the Nicholas Brothers, featuring Harold and Fayard, perform on two pedestals.

paced taps in 1932 at the Cotton Club (The Nicholas Brothers, n.d.). Fayard and Harold Nicholas grew up in Philadelphia and performed at the Cotton Club for 2 years. They went on to make several films including *Pie, Pie Blackbird* in 1932 and Broadway productions such as *Ziegfeld Follies* (1936).

Bill "Bojangles" Robinson, born in Richmond, Virginia, was best known for portraying an antebellum butler dancing opposite of Shirley Temple in movies such as *The Little Colonel* and *The Littlest Rebel* (Dubas 2006). His career began as a hoofer (see Hoofing, later in this chapter), and at the age of 50 he performed for the first time to a white audience as the first African American to dance with a white dancer. He wore wooden-soled and split-soled shoes, which allowed flexibility of foot movement. His cool, reserved style, busy feet, and expressive face along with his famous invention of the stair dance made him one of the great tappers on the stage and in films (Frank 1994).

No other dancer in the 1930s brought more little girls into dance studios everywhere to learn tap than **Shirley Temple**. She was one of the top money-making stars of the mid-1930s and the number one box office star from 1936 to 1938 (Dubas 2006). She performed with other great tap dancers such as Bill Robinson and Buddy Ebsen. She starred in 14 short films, 43 feature films, and over 25 storybook movies. Her career spanned from 1931 to 1961 (Dubas 2006).

John William Sublett, better known as **John W. Bubbles**, and performance partner **Ford L. "Buck" Washington** formed a team called Buck and Bubbles. Buck sang and played piano while Bubbles tap danced. They performed in *Broadway Frolics* (1922), *Blackbirds* (1930), and *Ziegfeld Follies* (1931). Bubbles' tap style emphasized percussive heel drops with unique accents and syncopations while cutting the tempo to extend the rhythm past eight beats (Frank 1994). This eccentric dance style earned him the title of father of rhythm tap, which was later called jazz tap.

Eleanor Powell started her Broadway career in *The Optimists* in 1928 and out of necessity learned to tap dance. Her machine-gun footwork gained her the title of world champion and the queen of tap. She danced opposite Fred Astaire in *Broadway Melody* and was considered by many to be the only partner of Astaire to outdance him.

Howard "Sandman" Sims, a vaudeville Apollo Theater tap dancer, was best known for using a sandbox full of sand to amplify his step sounds. He appeared in an episode of *The Cosby Show* (1990) in which he and Bill Cosby challenged each other in tap dance. Sims was also featured in *No Maps on My Taps* (1979), *The Cotton Club* (1984), *Harlem Nights* (1989), and *Tap* (1989).

Charles (Chuck) Green, considered a jazz tap dancer, as a youth stuck bottle caps on his bare feet and performed on sidewalks for money (Hill n.d.b). He was part of the duet Chuck and Chuckles, which toured the United States, Europe, and Australia performing at Radio City Music Hall, the Apollo Theatre, Paramount Theatre, the Capitol Theatre, and the Palace Theatre. In 1944, Chuck succumbed to stress and was committed to a mental institution for 15 years. After his release in 1959, Green, still a tap dancer, created his own bebop style, adding new harmonies and rhythmic patterns, and continued performing for stage and television.

Samuel George (Sammy) Davis, Jr. was a recording artist and a television and film star as well as a member of Frank Sinatra's Rat Pack. He was called Mr. Entertainer. As a child he performed on Broadway and in Las Vegas. In 1954 Davis lost his eye in an automobile accident. He starred on Broadway in *Mr. Wonderful* (1956) and *Golden Boy* (1964). Davis' television and film career included *Ocean's 11* (1960) and his variety show *The Sammy Davis, Jr. Show*. In 1972 he had a recording hit, "The Candy Man".

Jimmy Slyde, known as the *king of slides*, executed a skatelike hoofer. Slyde performed regularly with Duke Ellington and Count Basie in the 1940s and 1950s. His film career consisted of *The Cotton Club* (1984), *Tap* (1989), and *Round Midnight* (1986). Slyde also performed in the musical *Black and Blue* (1985).

Frederick Austerlitz (**Fred Astaire**) and sister **Adele Astaire** started their professional career in 1905 when Fred was 6 years old and Adele was 9 years old (Frank 1994). They appeared in *Lady Be Good* (1924), *Funny Face* (1927), and *The Band Wagon* (1931). Fred started a solo career in 1932 when Adele got married, and he later made 10 films with his famous dance partner **Ginger Rogers**. Some include *The Gay Divorcee* (1935), *Top Hat* (1935), *Follow the Fleet* (1936), and *Swing Time* (1936). Although he was known as a tap dancer, he rarely wore tap shoes during his performances.

Fred Astaire and Ginger Rogers are one of the most famous dance couples.

Virginia Katherine McMath (Ginger Rogers), best known as Fred Astaire's dance partner, made over 73 films (Frank 1994). Rogers had a career after Astaire and went on to win an Academy Award for Best Actress in *Kitty Foyle* (1940).

The title of *speed tapper* goes to Johnnie Lucille Collier, better known as **Ann Miller**. Inspired by Eleanor Powell and discovered by Lucille Ball,

DID YOU KNOW? ▶▶▶▶▶▶▶▶▶

Ginger Rogers may not have been the dancer that her partner Fred Astaire was, but she could act the part. Some people have said that her tap sounds in film were dubbed over because they were not clear and also that their music was dubbed over their live performance.

Miller started dancing to strengthen her legs from rickets (Frank 1994). Although she was known as a speed tapper in films, tap sounds were looped in later using a tap board because stage floors were too slick for taps. However, in 1946, a contest between Ann Miller and a typist determined which taps were faster. Ann Miller tapped 627 taps per minute compared to Ruth Myers, the typist, who typed 584 taps per minute (Frank 1994). The Guinness World Record for the most taps per minute is 1,163; it was achieved by Anthony Morigerato in Albany, New York, on June 23, 2011 (Guinness World Records 2011).

Gregory Hines started dancing with older brother Maurice; they were known as the Hines Brothers. They both made their Broadway debut in *The Girl in Pink Tights* (1954). Gregory went on to earn Tony Award nominations for *Eubie* (1979), *Comin' Uptown* (1980), and *Sophisticated Ladies* (1981), and he won a Tony Award for *Jelly's Last Jam* (1992). Gregory Hines is considered the greatest tap dancer of his generation. His first film role was in Mel Brooks' comedy *History of the World, Part I* (1981). He also had the leading role in *The Cotton Club* (1984), *White Nights* (1985), and *Running Scared* (1996). Hines also performed in *Tap* (1989) and *A Rage in Harlem* (1991). He had an Emmy Award nomination for his role in the 2001 mini-series *Bojangles* and his own sitcom *The Gregory Hines Show* (1997). Some dance scholars described his style as percussive phrasing of a musical composer while executing the lines of a dancer.

Other well-known tap dancers are **Bunny Briggs**, who Duke Ellington once said was "the most superleviathonic, rhythmaturgically-syncopated tapsthamatician-isamist" (Hill n.d.a). Briggs performed in the 1985 NBC special *Motown Returns*

Gregory Hines is considered the greatest tap dancer of his generation.

to the Apollo and the film *Tap* (1989), and he was nominated for a Tony Award in 1989 for *Black and Blue*.

Buddy Ebsen, better known as the character Jed Clampett in *The Beverly Hillbillies* (1962-1971), who also starred as detective Barnaby Jones in *Barnaby Jones* in the 1970s, was originally cast as the Tin Man in *The Wizard of Oz* (1939). He became very ill because of an allergic reaction to the powdered aluminum makeup.

What happens when you are taught by some of the great tap legends and their styles and training mold you into one of the greatest contemporary tappers? You become the *tap dance kid*, **Savion Glover**. Glover starred in *The Tap Dance Kid* (1983) when he was 10 years old, and he continued his Broadway career with *Black and Blue* (1989) and *Jelly's Last Jam* (1992). He won a Tony Award for *Bring in 'da Noise, Bring in 'da Funk* (1996). His film career included *Bamboozled* (2000) and *Happy Feet* (2006). He was a regular on *Sesame Street* (1991-1995). Currently, Glover is trying to bring back the old style and restore African roots to tap. Most recently, his performance in *SoLe Sanctuary* pays his respects to the craft of tap dance. Some say that Glover is the future of tap dance.

Savion Glover, considered by some to be the future of tap dance, is bringing back the old style and restoring African roots to tap.

Whether mentioned in this section or not, each person involved in tap has contributed to the evolution of this art form with his or her style, form, and creative movement.

STYLES AND AESTHETICS OF TAP DANCE

Throughout the history of tap dance, tap dancers have created many styles and aesthetics. Some dancers have even combined other forms of dance and art to create their own style. Eccentric dancing, which includes acrobatics, snake hips, the shimmy, and any other form of contortionist movements or comedy dance, was first introduced in the style called legomania, or rubber legs (Frank 1994). Incorporating high kicks, legomania is best known (although not a tap dance number) in the 1939 film *The Wizard of Oz,* where the scarecrow, played by Ray Boger, made it famous in the performance of "If I Only Had a Brain" (Frank 1994).

Soft-Shoe

Soft-shoe, a light, graceful dance performed in a smooth, leisurely cadence in soft-soled shoes, was made famous on the vaudeville stage (Frank 1994). One of the most famous soft-shoe routines is in *Bugs Bunny Rides Again* (Freleng 1948), where Yosemite Sam starts shooting at Bugs Bunny's feet while telling him to dance. Bugs Bunny grabs a hat and cane and starts dancing the soft-shoe, and he soon tricks Yosemite Sam into dancing with him. Sam quickly breaks into the same dance, and he is tricked into dancing into an open mine shaft.

Buck and Wing

Buck and wing is a flashy dance combining Irish and British clog, African rhythm, and fast footwork and kicks (Frank 1994). The term *buck* comes from buck dancers who wore wooden soles and danced on the balls of their feet, emphasizing movement below the waist. This form is similar to a clog dance, but it is much older. The term *wing* comes from the ballet term meaning *pigeon wing*: ailes de pigeon, also known as pistolet and brisé volé (Frank 1994). Other tap dancers developed a style that incorporated jazz and ballet movement using more upper-body movements.

Classical Tap

Classical tap, also referred to as *flash* or *swing tap*, was made famous by the Nicholas Brothers, who combined tap, ballet, and jazz dance with acrobatics. This style combined upper-body movement, wild and wiggly leg movements, and sensational acrobatic stunts with percussive, syncopated footwork.

Class Acts

Unlike the acrobatics of classical tap, **class acts** during the turn of the 20th century were more refined. Gymnastics, splits, and flips were rarely performed in this style. This style was dominated by **Honi Coles** and **Cholly Atkins**, who perfected the high-speed yet elegant close-to-the-floor style. They were known for their classic slow soft-shoe followed by a challenge dance where each would demonstrate swinging, percussive, complex steps along with a drummer.

Jazz Tap

When ragtime music (1897 and 1918) was featured in carnivals and circuses, tap dance transformed into syncopated jazz rhythms, called **jazz tap**. This style emphasizes precision, lightness, and speed. During the jazz age (1920s), tap dancers performed in front of swing or jazz bands with upright bodies. This became one of the fastest tap styles.

Hoofing

Hoofing is described as dancing into the floor with emphasis placed on stomps and stamps along with rhythmic percussions of the sounds, music, and syncopations. Savion Glover is a contemporary hoofer; he states that tap dance is a *dance* style, while hoofing is a *life*style.

Rhythm Tap

Rhythm tap, made famous by John W. Bubbles, incorporated more percussive heel drops and lower-body movement rather than emphasizing toe taps and upper-body movement. It is more grounded and focuses more on acoustic rather than the aesthetic qualities. Gregory Hines brought back this style, incorporating both finesse and grace and demonstrating that rhythm tap's focus is always on the feet.

Musical or Broadway Tap

Also known as *show tap,* the **musical or Broadway tap** style combines Hollywood with traditional forms of tap. Its main focus is on the performance along with body formations. Broadway musicals such as *Anything Goes, My One and Only,* and the most popular *42nd Street* showcase this style.

Funk Tap

This emerging style of tap combines hip hop with funk to create a contemporary, fun dance form. **Funk tap** is attracting a new generation of tap enthusiasts while preserving traditional tap technique.

Each style evolved from the many dancers that created these forms. These styles will continue to evolve as the next generation of tap dancers find and create their own style.

SUMMARY

Tap dance was not created at once; it has evolved, as have so many forms of dance. It took thousands of years to perfect it, and its future is in the hands of some of today's greatest dancers. Although its popularity in the movies peaked in the 1930s and 1940s, online video is still producing some wonderful tap stars, choreography, and talent. Tap dance has a rich history and a bright future as great teachers pass their taps down to their students.

To find supplementary materials for this chapter such as learning activities, e-journaling assignments, and web links, visit the web resource at www.HumanKinetics.com/BeginningTapDance1E.

Glossary

accent—Stress on the beat to make it strong or weak.

action words—Words that describe body actions (legs, arms, and head movements in the sequence of execution) during an exercise or step.

agility—Ability to change body positions and directions.

anatomical position—An erect standing position with the feet forward, arms down by the sides, and palms forward with the thumbs outward and fingers extended.

appendicular skeleton—Bones of the limbs.

Astaire, Adele—The older sister of Fred Astaire. They performed as partners until Adele got married in 1932.

Astaire, Fred—Born Frederick Austerlitz. Started his career with his sister Adele and later partnered with Ginger Rogers. Known as a tap dancer but rarely wore tap shoes.

Atkins, Cholly—Famous class acts performer who perfected the high-speed yet elegant close-to-the-floor style.

axial skeleton—Includes the skull, vertebral column, sternum, and ribs.

balance—Ability to maintain the body in proper equilibrium.

barre—A wooden or metal rail attached to several walls of the studio, or it may be a free-standing portable structure placed in the center of the studio.

Bates, Peg Leg—Considered the most famous one-legged dancer ever.

beat (pulse)—Basic unit of rhythmic organization or pulsation.

body awareness—Knowledge about how your body moves, along with body control, weight transfer, and balance.

Briggs, Bunny—Performed in the 1985 NBC special *Motown Returns to the Apollo* and was a 1989 Tony Award nominee for *Black and Blue*.

Brown, King Rastus—Considered one of the greatest buck dancers in the New York area in 1903.

Bryant, Willie—Invented the Shim Sham Shimmy routine with partner Leonard Reed.

Bubbles, John W.—Born John William Sublett. Part of the team Buck and Bubbles. He danced a tap style that emphasized percussive heel drops with unique accents and syncopations. His style earned him the title of father of rhythm tap.

buck and wing—A flashy dance combining Irish and British clog using African rhythm.

cardiorespiratory endurance—Ability of the lungs, heart, and blood vessels to deliver oxygen to all the cells in the body.

cartilaginous joints—Joints that are held together by cartilage (e.g., the intervertebral discs of the spinal column).

center—Part of the class in which students learn steps to gain a basic movement vocabulary of tap.

Chaplin, Charlie—Famous clog dancer who performed in a troupe called Seven Lancashire Lads in 1897.

class acts—A style of tap dance performed during the turn of the 20th century that was more refined than the classical tap style, without gymnastics, splits, and flips.

classical tap—Dance style that combines tap, ballet, and jazz dance with acrobatics; also referred to as *flash* or *swing tap*.

Coles, Honi—Famous class acts performer who perfected this high-speed yet elegant close-to-the-floor style of tap.

combination—Movement phrase consisting of several steps.

concentric—Shortening of muscle and visible joint movement.

coordination—Integration of the nervous and muscular systems to perform harmonious body movements.

Covan, Willie—Performed in minstrel shows with his future wife, brother, and friend, a group known as the Four Covans. He is credited with creating the rhythm waltz clog.

dance—Longer, more comprehensive movement series that typically lasts 2 to 4 minutes. Also called a *routine*.

Davis, Jr., Samuel George (Sammy)—A member of Frank Sinatra's Rat Pack, he starred in this own variety show and recorded the hit "Candy Man."

direction—Also known as line of motion; you can create it by moving through space in a circle, forward, sideways, or backward.

downbeat—Accent in a measure that is on the first beat.

dynamic (isotonic) muscle contraction—Occurs when the length of the involved muscle changes.

Ebsen, Buddy—Best known as the character Jed Clampett in *The Beverly Hillbillies* and as Barnaby Jones in the series of the same title.

eccentric—Tension involved in the lengthening of muscle.

fibrous joints—Joints that are tightly held together so that little to no true movement exists in them.

FITT principle—Acronym for frequency, intensity, time, and type of activity performed.

flexibility—Ability of the joint to move freely through the full range of motion.

flexibility exercises—Exercises performed to increase the range of motion at the joint. These stretching exercises are held for 15 to 30 seconds to ensure that muscle length increases.

flow—Sustained movement; a constant flow of smooth energy.

force—In movement, the release or compression of energy, the pull of gravity, and the sensation of heavy or light.

funk tap—Combines hip hop with funk to create a contemporary, fun dance form.

Glover, Savion—Starred in *The Tap Dance Kid* (1983) and won a Tony Award for *Bring in 'da Noise, Bring in 'da Funk*. He was the feet in *Happy Feet* (2006) and is considered the future of tap dance.

Green, Charles (Chuck)—Considered a jazz tap dancer, he created his own bebop style, adding new harmonies and rhythmic patterns.

health-related fitness components—Cardiorespiratory endurance (aerobic), muscular strength and endurance, flexibility, and body composition.

Hines, Gregory—Started dancing with his brother Maurice as the Hines Brothers. He is considered the greatest tap dancer of his generation.

hoofing—Dancing into the floor with emphasis placed on stomps and stamps along with rhythmic percussions of the sounds, music, and syncopations.

instrumentals—Music with no vocals; it can come at the beginning, end, or in between any sections.

isolation exercises—Movements performed with some parts of the body while keeping other parts still.

jazz tap—This style emphasizes precision, lightness, and speed and is considered to be one of the fastest tap styles.

Keeler, Ruby—Considered the first tap dancing star of the silver screen. He performed in the film *42nd Street* in 1933.

Kemp, William—Jig performer in the 1600s. He is best known as the original Peter in the play *Romeo and Juliet*.

kinesthetic sense—Muscle, bone, and joint sense; being able to feel the body in space.

Lane, William Henry—Considered Master Juba. He began his career in Manhattan's Five Points and was one of the first African American performers to perform for a white audience.

legomania—A form of rubber legs style of dance, incorporating high kicks.

level—Refers to the dancer's body in space and the transfer of weight from the center of gravity; movement can be performed above the center of gravity (high) or below the center of gravity (low).

macronutrients—The major nutritional building blocks: carbohydrate, protein, and fat.

marking—Using small movements to indicate leg and arm movements of an exercise or combination.

measure—Music divided into units defined by a given number of beats of a given duration.

meter—Recurring pattern in music.

metronome—A practice tool or device that produces a steady beat.

Miller, Ann—Born Johnnie Lucille Collier. Held the title of speed tapper. She started dancing to strengthen her legs after enduring rickets.

muscular endurance—Ability of the muscle to keep repeating force over time.

muscular strength—Ability of the muscle to exert maximal force against a resistance.

musicality—Understanding of music; in dance, how execution of movement relates to the music.

musical or Broadway tap—This style combines Hollywood with traditional forms of tap with the main focus on performance; also known as *show tap*.

musical style (genre)—Musical sounds that belong to a category.

Nicholas Brothers—Fayard and Harold Nicholas performed at the Cotton Club in 1932 and made the film *Pie, Pie Blackbird* and the Broadway production *Ziegfeld Follies*.

notes—Symbols that represent sounds.

note values—Symbols that represent the duration of sound.

overload principle—The body needs greater than normal stress, or load, to become stronger.

After a period of time the body adapts to this stress, and greater stress will need to be added for further gains.

performance attitude—Thinking, acting, and moving like a dancer.

personal space—Accommodates leg, arm, and body extensions without invading your neighbor's space while standing in one place or moving around the space.

phrasing—Occurs in music or tap when the pattern separates, or gets out of phase, and then rejoins, or gets back in sync, with the original pattern.

pitch—Frequency at which sound vibrates.

plié—To bend the knees.

Powell, Eleanor—Considered the queen of tap and considered the only partner to outdance Fred Astaire.

power—Ability to produce maximum force in a short period of time.

pre–warm-up—Exercises performed to prepare you physically and mentally for the dance class.

PRICED—Protection, rest, ice, compression, elevation, and diagnosis; aids in recovery from minor injuries.

prone position—Lying facedown on the stomach.

range—Amount of space the body fills as it moves in pathways either on the floor or in the air (straight, curved, zigzag, spiral, or wavy).

reaction time—Time required to initiate a response to a stimulus.

Reed, Leonard—Invented the Shim Sham Shimmy routine with partner Willie Bryant.

relationship awareness—Can include body parts, people, and objects; what and to whom the body relates.

rest sign—A symbol in musical notation that represents silence.

rhythm—Measured movement and the timing of notes.

rhythm tap—A style of tap dance characterized by percussive heel drops and lower-body movement.

Rice, Thomas Dartmouth "Daddy"—Developed the song and dance routine of the exaggerated, highly stereotyped African American character called "Jim Crow" and went on to be known as the father of American minstrelsy.

Robinson, Bill "Bojangles"—Best known for the invention of the stair dance and is considered one of the great tappers on stage and films.

Rogers, Ginger—Born Virginia Katherine McMath. Best known as Fred Astaire's partner but later went on to win an Academy Award for best actress in *Kitty Foyle* (1940).

routine—See *dance*.

Sims, Howard "Sandman"—Vaudeville Apollo Theater tap dancer best known for using a large box full of sand to amplify his step sounds.

skill-related fitness components—Coordination, agility, balance, power, reaction time, and speed.

Slyde, Jimmy—Known as the king of slides for executing a skatelike hoofer.

soft-shoe—A light, graceful dance performed in a smooth and leisurely cadence with soft-soled shoes.

spatial sense—A sense that is based on the knowledge that everyone occupies space and any movement defines internal body space and general space.

speed—Ability to propel the body from one place to another.

sprain—Injury by tearing of a ligament or other joint tissue.

staff—The five horizontal lines and four spaces in musical notation; each line or space represents a different pitch.

strain—Injury by overstretching and tearing of a muscle or tendon fiber.

supine position—Lying faceup on the back.

syncopation—Accenting the offbeat in a measure.

synovial joints—Allow for the most freedom of movement and are the most common joints.

technique—Includes not only correct performance but also incorporation of movement principles that apply to the exercise or the step in a combination.

Temple, Shirley—One of the top money-making stars of the mid-1930s and the top box office star from 1936 to 1938. She performed with Bill Robinson and Buddy Ebsen.

tempo—The speed of the beat or speed of movement.

time—Inner rhythms of breath or pulse or external rhythmic elements of tempo.

time signature (meter signature)—Notation used to specify how many beats are in each measure and which note value constitutes one beat.

Washington, Ford L. "Buck"—Part of the team Buck and Bubbles. He played the piano while Bubbles tap danced.

References
and Resources

Adams, M. 2011. *Lee de Forest: King of radio, television, and film.* New York: Copernicus Books.

Alan, M. 2007. Tall tales but true? New York's "five points" slums. *Journal of Urban History* Vol. 33(2): pp. 320-331.

Alpert, P.T. 2011. The health benefits of dance. *Home Health Care Management & Practice* Vol. 23(2): pp. 155-157.

Asante, K.W. 2002. *African dance: An artistic, historical, and philosophical inquiry.* Trenton, NJ: Africa World Press Inc.

Baechle, T.R., & R.W. Earle. (Eds.) 2003. *Essentials of strength training and conditioning.* Champaign, IL: Human Kinetics.

Benton, L. 2011. Abolition and imperial law, 1790-1820. *Journal of Imperial & Commonwealth History* Vol. 39(3): pp. 355-374.

Bingaman, M. 2011. Native American dance history. www.ehow.com/about_6136173_native-american-dance-history.html#ixzz1fWIdD33I.

Blood, B. 2011. Music theory online: Tempo lesson 5. Dolmetsch Organisation. www.dolmetsch.com/musictheory5.htm.

Brashers-Krug, T., R. Shadmehr, & E. Bizzi. 1996. Consolidation in human motor memory. *Nature* Vol. 382: pp. 252-255.

Brehm, M., & C. Kampfe. 1997. Creative dance improvisation: Fostering creative expression, group cooperation, and multiple intelligences. www.eric.ed.gov/contentdelivery/servlet/ERICServlet?accno=ED425401.

Burrows, T. 1999. *How to read music: Reading music made simple.* New York: St. Martin's Press.

Cherokee stomp dance. n.d. Retrieved from www.aaanativearts.com/cherokee/cherokee-stomp-dance.htm.

Clippinger, K. 2007. *Dance anatomy and kinesiology.* Champaign, IL: Human Kinetics.

Collier, J.P. 1853. *Lives of the original actors in Shakespeare's plays.* London: Shakespeare Society.

Cone, T.C., & S.L. Cone. 2005. *Teaching children dance.* 2nd ed. Champaign, IL: Human Kinetics.

Cuypers, K. 2011. *Good Housekeeping.* November. http://besteducationpossible.blogsport.com/2011/10/tickets-to-health-and-happiness.html.

Dimondstein, G., & N.W. Prevots. 1969. Development of a dance curriculum for young children. CAREL Arts and Humanities Curriculum Development Program for Young Children. Retrieved from www.eric.ed.gov/ERICWebPortal/contentdelivery/servlet/ERICServlet?accno=ED032936.

Dixon, S., F. Gouyon, & G. Widmer. 2003. *Towards characterization of music via rhythmic patterns.* Austrian Research Institute for AI. Vienna, Austria: Fabien Gouyon Universitat Pompeu Fabra.

Donald, G. 1977. Native American slavery in the Southern colonies. *Indian Historian* 10(2): pp. 38-42.

Dubas, R. 2006. *Shirley Temple: A pictorial history of the world's greatest child star.* New York: Applause Theatre & Cinema Books.

Dunford, M. (Ed.) 2006. *Sports nutrition: A practice manual for professionals.* 5th ed. Chicago: American Dietetic Association.

Elliott, G.H. 1997. *An investigation into a movement education program on motor creativity in preschool children in inclusive and general physical education environments.* Columbus: Ohio State University.

Evans, R. 1978. *How to read music: Fundamentals of music notation made easy.* New York: Three Rivers Press.

Feldman, A. 1996. *Inside tap: Technique and improvisation for today's tap dancer.* Pennington, NY: Princeton Books.

Frank, R. 1994. *Tap! The greatest tap dance stars and their stories 1900-1955.* New York: Da Capo Press.

Freleng, F. (Director). 1948. *Bugs Bunny rides again* [Motion picture]. United States: Warner Brothers.

Gallay, A. 2003. *The Indian slave trade: The rise of the English Empire in the American South 1670-1717.* New Haven, CT: Yale University Press.

Gilbert, A. 1998. *Al Gilbert's tap dictionary: The world of tap at your fingertips!* Laguna Beach, CA: Music Works.

Gray, A. 1998. *The souls of your feet: A tap dance guidebook for rhythm explorers.* Austin, TX: Grand Weavers.

Guinness World Records. 2011. Most taps in a minute. www.guinnessworldrecords.com/records-3000/tap-dancing-most-taps-in-a-minute.

Harnum, J. 2009. *Basic music theory: How to read, write, and understand written music.* Anchorage: Sol Ut Press.

Hill, C.V. 2010. *Tap dancing American: A cultural history.* London: Oxford University Press.

Hill, C.V. n.d.a. Bunny Briggs. Retrieved from www.atdf.org/awards/bunny.html.

Hill, C.V. n.d.b. Chuck Green. Retrieved from www.atdf.org/awards/green.html.

Hill, C.V., & S. Sommer. 2006. Tap dance. In *Encyclopedia of African American culture and history.* 2nd ed. C.A. Palmer (Ed.). Vol. 5: pp. 2163-2167.

Inglehearn, M. 1993. The hornpipe: Our national dance. Papers from a conference held at Sutton House, Homerton, London E9 6JQ. http://chrisbrady.itgo.com/dance/stepdance/hornpipe_conference.htm.

Jeannerod, M. 1994. The representing brain: Neural correlates of motor intention and imagery. *Behavioral and Brain Sciences* 17: pp. 187-202.

Kassing, G., & D.M. Jay. 2003. *Dance teaching methods and curriculum design.* Champaign, IL: Human Kinetics.

Kenrick, J. 2011. *History of musical films.* Musicals 101.com. The Cyber Encyclopedia of Musical Theatre, TV and Film. www.musicals101.com/index.html.

Knowles, M. 2002. *Tap roots: The early history of tap dancing.* Jefferson, NC: McFarland.

Liggett, L. 1998. The Wounded Knee Massacre: An introduction. American Culture Studies Program. www.bgsu.edu/departments/acs/1890s/woundedknee/WKIntro.html.

Litwack, L.F. 2006. Jim Crow. In *Encyclopedia of African American culture and history.* 2nd ed. C.A. Palmer (Ed.). Vol. 3: pp. 1176-1178.

Meyer, T., X.L. Qi, T.R. Stanford, & C. Constantinidis. 2011. Stimulus selectivity in dorsal and ventral prefrontal cortex after training in working memory task. *Journal of Neuroscience* 31(17): pp. 6266-6276.

National Dance Teachers Association. n.d. Advice & information: Dance studio specification. Retrieved from www.ndta.org.uk/advice-information/dance-studio-specification.

New World Encyclopedia. n.d. African dance. Retrieved from www.newworldencyclopedia.org/entry/African_dance.

The Nicholas Brothers. n.d. Retrieved from www.nicholasbrothers.com/index.htm.

Oxford, E. 1996. The great famine. *American History* 31(1): p. 52.

Perpich Center for Arts Education. 2009. The elements of dance. Retrieved from www.opd.mpls.k12.mn.us/The_Elements_of_Dance.html.

Pittman, A.M., M.S. Waller, & C.L. Dark. 2009. *Dance a while.* San Francisco: Pearson Education.

Rowan, J. 2003. Al Gilbert: The free library. Retrieved from www.thefreelibrary.com/Al Gilbert.-a0108114349.

Saito, E.T., P.M.H. Hanai Akashi, & I.C. Neves Sacco. 2009. Global body posture evaluation in patients with temporomandibular joint disorder. *Clinics* 64(1). www.scielo.br/scielo.php?pid=S1807-59322009000100007&script=sci_arttext.

Toll, R.C. 2006. Minstrels/Minstrelsy. In *Encyclopedia of African American culture and history.* 2nd ed. C.A. Palmer (Ed.). Vol. 4: pp. 1456-1459.

Tracey, P. 1993. The Lancashire. Papers from a conference held at Sutton House, Homerton, London E9 6JQ. http://chrisbrady.itgo.com/dance/stepdance/hornpipe_conference.htm.

Van't Hof, E. 2002. "Essence" dance: A simple model for improvisation. Retrieved from www.eric.ed.gov/ERICWebPortal/detail?accno=ED464905.

Vetter, R.E., S.A. Myllykangas, L.K.M. Donorfio, & A.K. Foose. 2011. Creative movements as a stress-reduction intervention for caregivers. *Journal of Physical Education, Recreation and Dance* 82(2): pp. 35-38.

Wood, P.H. 2006. Stono Rebellion. In *Encyclopedia of African American culture and history*. 2nd ed. C.A. Palmer (Ed.). Vol. 5: pp. 2149-2150.

Yenerall, K. 2009. Jim Crow laws. In *Encyclopedia of American government and civics*. M.A. Genovese & L.C. Han (Eds.). New York: Facts on File. Library of American History. pp. 176-180.

Index

Note: The italicized *f* following page numbers refers to figures.

About the Author

Lisa Lewis, PhD, is an associate professor in the health and human performance department at Austin Peay State University in Tennessee. Originally from North Carolina, Dr. Lewis started her professional dance training under master teachers Mallory Graham and Danny Hoctor, and later she studied in New York City under the legendary jazz teacher Frank Hatchett and tap professional Maurice Hines at Hines-Hatchett studio (currently Broadway Dance Center). Dr. Lewis developed online tap dance components for beginners while instructing tap dance at Middle Tennessee State University.

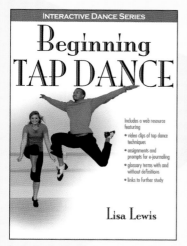
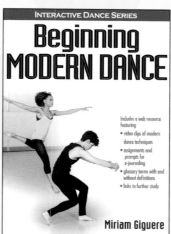
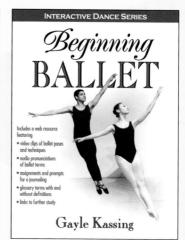

You'll find other outstanding
dance resources at
www.HumanKinetics.com

In the U.S. call 1.800.747.4457
Australia 08 8372 0999
Canada. 1.800.465.7301
Europe . . . . .+44 (0) 113 255 5665
New Zealand 0800 222 062

HUMAN KINETICS
The Information Leader in Physical Activity & Health
P.O. Box 5076 • Champaign, IL 61825-5076